Higher

MATHEMATICS
GCSE for Edexcel
Problem-solving Book

Tabitha Steel, Coral Thomas, Mark Dawes and Steven Watson

CAMBRIDGE
UNIVERSITY PRESS

University Printing House, Cambridge CB2 8BS, United Kingdom

Cambridge University Press is part of the University of Cambridge.

It furthers the University's mission by disseminating knowledge in the pursuit of
education, learning and research at the highest international levels of excellence.

www.cambridge.org
Information on this title:
www.cambridge.org/ukschools/9781107450059 (Paperback)

© Cambridge University Press 2015

First published 2015

Printed in the United Kingdom by Latimer Trend

A catalogue record for this publication is available from the British Library

ISBN 978-1-107-45005-9 Paperback

Additional resources for this publication at www.cambridge.org/ukschools

Cover image © 2013 Fabian Oefner www.fabianoefner.com

Contents

Introduction   iv

Problem-solving strategies: 1–110

1   Draw a diagram   1
2   I can't do that but I can do this   16
3   Adding lines   30
4   Solve a simpler problem   43
5   Make changes to the problem   53
6   Do you recognise the problem?   61
7   What is a sensible answer?   73
8   It depends how you look at it   82
9   Work systematically   95
10 If you don't know what to do, do something   102

Worked solutions: 111–232

1   Draw a diagram   111
2   I can't do that but I can do this   128
3   Adding lines   141
4   Solve a simpler problem   157
5   Make changes to the problem   165
6   Do you recognise the problem?   176
7   What is a sensible answer?   187
8   It depends how you look at it   195
9   Work systematically   210
10 If you don't know what to do, do something   218

Introduction

What is a mathematical problem?

In everyday speech you might talk about a 'problem' as being something that is negative and often annoying. It might also be referred to as a difficulty, or as something that needs to be fixed.

Mathematical problems might be difficult, they might even be annoying, but they are certainly not negative! Some people see mathematical problems as any sort of mathematical question and some people use 'problem' in this way. 2 + 3 is quite a simple question. 117 × 495 is more difficult but it is still just a question (even though some people will not know how to work it out).

The definition of a mathematical problem used in this book is: something you don't know how to solve immediately.

117 × 495 could be worked out by writing down the number 117, adding on 117, and adding on another 117 again and again until you have written it 495 times. Even if you don't have a quicker way of working this out (and it would be a good idea to have a quicker way!) then this is not actually mathematical problem-solving.

You often need to think 'around' a problem before you can get started.

A mathematical problem, then, is likely to be challenging, and it might well be the case that you can't 'see' the answer quickly. There are lots of things that might help you though, and this book will show you some of those ideas.

Different types of mathematics

To be able to do maths you need to know and understand mathematical ideas. These are important, and Cambridge University Press's *GCSE Mathematics for Edexcel Higher Student Book* covers this sort of material. You also need to be able to solve problems, and this can be more difficult.

Problem-solving 'muscle memory'

When you learn to do something new you usually have to think very hard about what you are doing. For example, when someone first learns to drive a car they have to concentrate hard and decide which foot to press down, which way to move the gear stick, which mirror to look in, and so on. Experienced motorists still need to concentrate on the road, but they don't need to think about the mechanics of every single action they take. This is known as 'muscle memory'. Muscle memory comes up lots in sports, so a footballer might have to train hard to learn how to do a rainbow flick, but will then be able to do it without thinking about it.

When you solve an equation the answer itself is often not very exciting ("$x = 3$... big deal!"). The important thing when solving lots of equations is not finding out whether x happens to be 3 or 4 this time around, but that you are putting equation-solving in your muscle memory. Some of the problems you solve in this book **will** be interesting in their own right. We hope you will enjoy the challenge of doing them and will enjoy the answers too. Beyond this, though, you should not just work out the answers and be satisfied with that. After each problem, try to reflect on how you solved it. It is important to think about this, because this is the point at which you will learn new skills and this is how the muscle memory will start to develop.

Impossible to obvious

At first, a mathematical problem may appear to be impossible. When you know the answer or when you know how to do it, the problem can then seem obvious and not worth thinking about.

Hopefully you will avoid both of these extremes. None of the problems you will be asked to solve in this book are 'impossible' – do see them as a challenge. Even if a problem is obvious to you it is still likely to involve important ideas that you might be able to apply to other, more challenging problems in the future.

> *Year 3000* by *Busted* has the chorus lyric:
>
> "I've been to the year 3000. ...
>
> And your great, great, great granddaughter
>
> Is pretty fine."
>
> You might be concerned about the number of 'great's in the lyric.
>
> How do we know we need more 'great's? How many 'great's should there be?

Start working on this problem by yourself. Once you've finished, talk to other people about what you have done.

How to use this book

Each chapter in this book covers a problem-solving strategy – a way of approaching a problem. The chapter starts by describing the strategy and how to apply it to a problem. This is followed by questions which you can solve by applying that strategy.

Each question covers one or more strands of maths, which is shown by the colour wheel beside the question number.

The exploded pieces(s) of the colour wheel tells you what strand(s) of maths each question covers:

Number

Algebra

Ratio, proportion and rates of change

Geometry and measures

Probability

Statistics

The questions have been written to give you regular practice at problem solving so that you can build your skills, confidence and mathematical experience not only for your GCSE exams but also for life outside the classroom.

The star rating suggests the amount of problem-solving experience needed to tackle each question.

⭐⭐⭐ 1 star questions are 'entry-level', they are good questions to start with.

⭐⭐⭐ 2 star questions are ideal to move on to when you have confidently and successfully completed some of the entry-level questions.

⭐⭐⭐ 3 star questions are for when you need more of a challenge.

In other words, the more stars, the more difficult the question is.

This means that you might need a calculator to work through the problem.

This means that you should work through a question without a calculator. If this symbol is not present, you can use a calculator if you want.

 Tip

Tip boxes provide hints to help you work through questions.

Worked solutions to all the questions are provided at the back of the book. Blue boxes next to the solutions guide you through the working.

There is an old saying: 'A picture is worth a thousand words'.

So, if a diagram is not provided then draw one. It might be helpful, and could give you some ideas about how to solve the problem.

Draw a decent diagram. A sketch is probably fine, but it needs to look like the scenario it describes. If there is a triangle in the problem then your shape should be a triangle. If there is supposed to be a straight line then your line should be straight. The actual sizes of sides and angles are probably not important. Try to make your diagrams large and clear.

Annotate your diagram. If there is information provided in the question (such as the lengths of sides, or the sizes of angles) then write these on your diagram. This will often help when you are solving a problem.

Add new information that you work out. When you work out something new, add this to the diagram too.

So, in summary:

- draw a decent diagram
- label it
- add new information that you work out.

It is fairly obvious what to do when a diagram has been provided as part of a question, but a diagram can sometimes be useful in other situations. Here are two examples where drawing diagrams could help you.

> At a fast food restaurant there is a 'meal deal' that involves first choosing one of the following: cheeseburger, chicken burger, veggie burger or salad, and then ordering a side from the following list: fries, baked potato or coleslaw.
>
> How many different meals could you have?

You could work systematically and create a list, but a diagram would also help.

The diagram above shows all the options and the lines show some of the possible combinations.

There are three lines coming from cheeseburger. How many lines will come from chicken burger when the diagram is finished? Will this help you answer the question?

Alternatively, you could create a table like the one below to help you. What does each cell in this table represent? How does this table tell you, at a glance, how many meal possibilities there are?

	Fries	Baked potato	Coleslaw
Cheeseburger			
Chicken burger			
Veggie burger			
Salad			

1	2	3	4	5	6
7	8	9	10	11	12
13	14	15	16	17	18
19	20	21	22	23	24
25	26	27	28	29	30
31	32	33	34	35	36
37	38	39	40	41	42
43	44	45	46	47	48
49	50	51	52	53	54
55	56	57	58	59	60
61	62	63	64	65	66
67	68	69	70	71	72
73	74	75	76	77	78
79	80	81	82	83	84
85	86	87	88	89	90
91	92	93	94	95	96

Here is another example:

Jilly says: 'If I write out numbers in rows of six, all of the prime numbers will either be in the top row, in the column that has 1 at the top or in the column that has 5 at the top.'

Can you tell if she is right?

You need to have some numbers to look at here so a diagram will be important.

Now you could start highlighting a few prime numbers.

This looks good so far. (It is worth noting that Jilly didn't say that every number in the top row would be prime, just that all of the primes would be in the top row or the 1 or 5 columns).

1	2	3	4	5	6
7	8	9	10	11	12
13	14	15	16	17	18
19	20	21	22	23	24
25	26	27	28	29	30
31	32	33	34	35	36

Now, why can't there be any prime numbers in the column with 2 at the top?

When you go down a row, it is the same as adding 6 to the number above. The 2 column goes: 2, 8, 14, 20, 26, and because you started with an even number and are adding an even number, these will always be even. So there can't be any more prime numbers in this column.

The column with 3 at the top has numbers that are all odd. But they are all multiples of 3.

The column with 4 at the top cannot have any prime numbers in it. Why not?

Neither can the column with 6 at the top.

This just leaves you with two columns and the top row for primes to go in. This means that Jilly is right.

The following problems may be solved using more than one method; however, the worked solutions provided at the back of this book are based on the method introduced above.

A rectangle has length $2x + 3$ and width $x - 1$.

a Write an expression for the perimeter of the rectangle.

b Write an expression for the area of the rectangle.

The perimeter of the rectangle is 70 cm.

c How long is the longest side?

d What is the area of the rectangle?

In a cement factory, the cement bags are placed on pallets made of planks of wood and bricks.

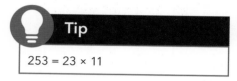

Tip

$253 = 23 \times 11$

The number of bricks needed to make the pallet is calculated as 'one more than the length of the plank in metres'.

a What length of pallet uses five bricks?

b If the pallet is 7 m long, how many bricks are used in it?

The factory needs pallets with a total length of 25 m for the next batch of cement. It has planks of wood that are 4 m long and 3 m long.

c What combinations of planks can they have?

d How many bricks would be needed for each combination?

Ann-Marie wants to plant a cherry tree in her garden. When it is fully grown it will have a diameter of 3 m.

Ann-Marie wants all of the fruit to fall on her lawn.

Here is a sketch, not drawn to scale, of Ann-Marie's garden.

Where could the tree be planted?

The diagram represents two remote towns A and B.

The mountain rescue helicopters from both towns are dispatched to rescue any casualty within a radius of 25 km of town A or town B. The fire brigade from town B will travel to any accident scene closer to town B than town A.

Shade the region that the helicopters and town B's and fire brigade will both cover.

The probability Leela catches the 6.30 am train to Brighton is 0.7.

If she misses the train she will be late for work.

The probability the train will be late is 0.15.

If the train is late she will be late for work.

What is the probability Leela will be on time for work on a particular day?

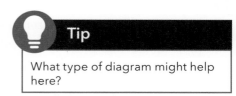

Tip

What type of diagram might help here?

Two five-sided spinners are numbered 1 to 5. When the arrows are spun, your total score is calculated by adding the two numbers the spinners land on.

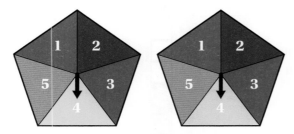

a Draw a suitable diagram to show all possible outcomes when spinning these spinners.

b What is the highest score you could get?

c What is probability of getting a total score of 8?

The vertices of a quadrilateral are A, B, C and D. A has coordinates (2, 1).
$\overrightarrow{AB} = \begin{pmatrix} 2 \\ 3 \end{pmatrix}$, $\overrightarrow{BC} = \begin{pmatrix} 4 \\ 0 \end{pmatrix}$, $\overrightarrow{AD} = \begin{pmatrix} 4 \\ 0 \end{pmatrix}$

a Write a column vector for $\overrightarrow{CD}$.

b Compare $\overrightarrow{CD}$ with $\overrightarrow{AB}$. What do you notice? Can you explain?

c What type of quadrilateral is $ABCD$?

Tip

Draw the shape on squared paper.

A projector is placed 1 m from a screen. When the projector is turned on, the image produced is only 20 cm high.

How far back should the projector be moved in order to produce an image that fills the screen, which is approximately 1.5 m in height? (Assume that no other adjustments are made to the projector.)

Peter the factory manager planned to install a new hot drinks machine for the factory workers. He decided to fill it with tea because he thought tea was the most popular hot drink.

Tip

What type of diagram might be helpful?

The workers did a survey to check their preferred hot drink. Each person could choose hot chocolate, tea or coffee.

8 women wanted hot chocolate. 16 workers wanted tea, of which 7 were men. 10 men and 12 women wanted coffee. There were 25 men in total.

Was Peter correct?

Mr Rixson and Mrs Lloyd are the A Level Mathematics teachers at Swanend Hill School. They are extremely competitive and often have debates about their students' results.

Tip

Draw a possible box plot for both classes.

The results from the latest assessments were as follows:

Class	Mean score	Median score	Range	IQR	Lowest score	Highest score
Rixson	7.5	7.5	9	4	3	12
Lloyd	9	7	17	14.5	1	18

Both Mr Rixson and Mrs Lloyd have 12 students in their A Level Mathematics classes.

Compare the results of the classes.

Marianne needs to make a long-distance journey. She is looking for the cheapest car hire.

Whacky Wheels has a standard charge of £35, then 15p for every kilometre driven.

Wheelies Rentals has a charge of £23 per 100 km travelled.

a Complete the charges graph for both car hire companies.

Tip

In this question you can use the axes that are given to help you draw the diagram.

b As Marianne thinks the return journey is 300 km, which company would be the cheaper to use?

c Marianne made a mistake in her route plan and the return journey was 500 km. Would Marianne have saved money by using the other hire company?

Granny Bessie is making a patchwork quilt with scraps of fabric.

Tip

The diagram in the question is very detailed. Could a simpler diagram help?

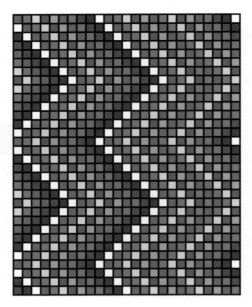

Each patch is $(2x - 3)$ cm long and $(x + 3)$ cm deep.

a There are 25 patches in each row. Write a possible expression for the width of the quilt.

b There are 32 patches in each column. Write a possible expression for the length of the quilt.

c Write an expression for the area of the quilt, in the form $m(ax^2 + bx + c)$ where m is a constant.

The area of the quilt is $2.8 \, \text{m}^2$.

Tip

$2.8 \, \text{m}^2 = 28\,000 \, \text{cm}^2$. It may be easier to work in centimetres.

d What are the dimensions of each patch? Give your answers in centimetres.

A square-based food container has a capacity of $1440 \, \text{cm}^3$.

The base of the container is of length x cm.

a Write an expression for the height of the container in terms of x.

The inside of the container (base and four sides) is to be lined with parchment paper, with no overlaps.

b What is the expression, in terms of x, for the total area of parchment paper needed?

c If the height of the container is 10 cm, what is the size of the base?

d What is the area of the parchment paper needed?

A rectangular swimming pool is surrounded by a path made of very decorative mosaic tiles. The width of the path is x.

The pool itself measures 35 m by 30 m.

a Write an expression for the area of the tile path in terms of x.

Having the tile path laid was very expensive.

It cost a total of £3196.80, at a rate of £30 per square metre.

b Find the width of the path to the nearest centimetre.

$ABCD$ is a field surrounded by fences AB, BC, CD and DA.

There is a dog tied to the spike X on a lead measuring 3 m.

There is a bull on an 8 m rope which is attached to the top of post A.

Find a route from corner D to corner B that would avoid both the bull and the dog.

Serrianne has taken up golf and goes to a golf range twice a week. She uses one bucket of balls each time. In every bucket of 25 balls there are always three yellow balls; the rest are white.

Serrianne hits one ball (chosen at random) at a time.

a What is the probability that the first three balls she uses will all be yellow?

b What is the probability that the first three balls she uses will all be white?

c Calculate the probability that the first three balls Serrianne uses are a mixture of two yellow and one white.

On his journey to work Abu must drive through two sets of traffic lights.

The probability of the first set being green is 0.7. If the first set is green the probability of the second set also being green is 0.8. But if the first set is not green the probability of the second set being green is 0.4.

a What is the probability that Abu does not have to stop on his journey to work tomorrow?

b What is the probability that Abu only has to stop once on his journey to work tomorrow?

Geoff and Ravinder are very competitive and often have badminton and squash matches. The probability of Geoff winning at badminton is 0.85 and the probability of Geoff winning at squash is 0.35.

a What is the probability that the next time they play both matches, Geoff wins both?

b What is the probability that Geoff loses at badminton but wins at squash?

c What is the probability that both boys win one match each?

On a commercial flight to Tanzania the passengers were questioned about their malaria precautions. Only 70% of the passengers had obtained and started a course of anti-malarial tablets. The chances of getting malaria are one in 200 if you take the tablets but one in 50 if you are not taking the tablets. What is the probability that one passenger selected randomly will catch malaria?

Tip

What type of diagram would be helpful?

A local bookshop was doing a survey on the most popular A Level courses to help decide how many revision guides to stock. 200 students were asked whether they studied Chemistry, Physics and Maths.

43 of the students surveyed did not study any of these three subjects.

92 were studying Chemistry.

23 were studying both Chemistry and Maths, but not Physics.

19 were studying both Physics and Maths, but not Chemistry.

29 were only studying Physics, and a total of 74 studied Physics.

53 of the students studied two of these three subjects.

a Display the information in an appropriate diagram.

b If one person was chosen at random, what is the probability they only studied maths?

c If one person was chosen at random, what is the probability they studied at least two of the subjects?

The point A has coordinates $(2, 2)$.

$\overrightarrow{AB} = \begin{pmatrix} 2 \\ 5 \end{pmatrix}$

$\overrightarrow{BC} = \begin{pmatrix} 3 \\ 0 \end{pmatrix}$

a Find a possible pair of coordinates for D, if $ABCD$ is an isosceles trapezium.

b Write $\overrightarrow{AC}$ as a column vector.

c Find the coordinates of E, if $\overrightarrow{AE} = 4\overrightarrow{BC}$.

d Using these coordinates for E, write $\overrightarrow{BE}$ as a column vector.

Tip

Draw a sketch of the shape.

Eve took a photo of her mum on holiday. Later, when Eve looks at the picture, she sees that her mum seems to be the same height as a hill in the background.

Eve stood approximately 3 m away from her mum when she took the photo, and they were approximately 2 km away from the hill. Eve's mum is 15 cm taller than Eve.

How tall is the hill?

When enlarging photographs, the increase in width and length must be directly proportional to each other or the photos will be distorted.

A photo has a width of 40 cm and a length of 55 cm.

a An enlargement has a width of 112 cm. Find its length.

b Another enlargement has a length of 148.5 cm. What must its width be?

c A third photo with a length of 15 cm and an area of 127.5 cm² is enlarged to a poster with a width of 25.5 cm. What is the area of this poster?

a Harriet has a challenge for her classmate Janet:

'I'm thinking of a triangle with a right angle. It has one angle of 40° and one side length of 5 cm.'

   i Accurately construct a triangle that satisfies Harriet's conditions.

   ii Demonstrate that there is more than one triangle that fulfils her conditions.

   iii How could Harriet alter her challenge so that only one triangle is possible?

b Janet comes up with a challenge for Harriet:

'My triangle has one side of length 4 cm and another that is 7 cm. The angle in between these two sides is 55°.'

   i How many triangles satisfy Janet's conditions? Explain your answer..

   ii Find the length of the third side.

Tip

To construct an accurate triangle you may need to use a ruler, protractor and a pair of compasses.

Tip

Before you start your accurate construction, make some sketches to show the positions of the sides and angles you are given.

Elspeth has an allotment. She is testing out two different types of grow bags for her tomato seedlings, which she gets to a healthy stage and then sells to her neighbours.

She has planted 20 seedlings in each bag. After three weeks she has recorded the heights of the plants as follows:

A   B

	Shortest height (cm)	Lower quartile (cm)	Median (cm)	IQR (cm)	Biggest height (cm)
Grow Bag A	5	12	15	8	22
Grow Bag B	8	13	15	5	25

a Compare the data.

b In your opinion, which type of grow bag is the best: A or B? Explain your choice.

Caroline and Janet do some swimming every day. They swim a total of 45 lengths each. They always start together but never finish together. They swim at different speeds for different swimming strokes.

Caroline always swims 45 lengths of breaststroke in 30 minutes, completing each one at the same speed.

Janet always does 30 lengths of front crawl in the first 12 minutes, then the remaining 15 lengths at a speed of one length per 40 seconds.

a After 10 minutes, how many lengths has Caroline completed?

b How long does it take Janet to complete her final 15 lengths?

c What is Caroline's speed in lengths per minute?

d How long must Janet wait for Caroline to finish?

e Roughly, on average, how many lengths does Janet swim each minute?

f If Caroline continued swimming for another 10 minutes, in theory how many lengths should she complete in total? Explain why this figure might not be correct.

27 ✪✪✪

Two of the vertices of an equilateral triangle are located at points with coordinates (0, 0) and (6, 0).

a Work out the possible coordinates of the third vertex.

b Instead, if two of the vertices of an equilateral triangle are located at (−3, 2) and (5, −4), what is its area?

28 ✪✪✪

Two astronomers want to calculate the distance to one of our closest stars, Alpha Centauri. In order to do so they take two angle measurements, six months apart. The two angles measured by the astronomers are shown in the diagrams on the right.

> 1 Astronomical Unit (AU) $\approx 1.5 \times 10^8$ km
>
> 1 arcsec $= (\frac{1}{3600})°$

Use the astronomers' measurements to calculate an approximate distance to Alpha Centauri.

You are 'armed' with the three transformations listed below:

A Reflect in the line $y = x$.

B Translate by $\begin{pmatrix} 1 \\ 0 \end{pmatrix}$.

C Enlarge by scale factor $\frac{1}{2}$ about the point $(2, 3)$.

Carry out all three transformations, in order, to a starting shape of your choice.

a How does the resulting image change if the transformations are applied in reverse order? $\mathbf{C} \longrightarrow \mathbf{B} \longrightarrow \mathbf{A}$

b How many different final images could be produced by changing the order in which the three transformations are applied?

Tip

You will find this question easier if you try it out. Think about how you can make it simpler by choosing (irregular) shapes and side lengths that make the enlargement easier.

With some problems, it is easier not to focus straightaway on the answer you need. Sometimes it is easier to work out what you **can** do and this might lead you to the answer almost by accident! Here is an example to demonstrate.

> In the diagram below, a square and an isosceles triangle sit on a straight line. Work out the size of angle *A*.

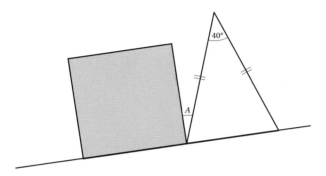

At the moment you can't work out angle *A*. But there are some things you **do** know.

There is a square in the diagram, so you can put in some angles.

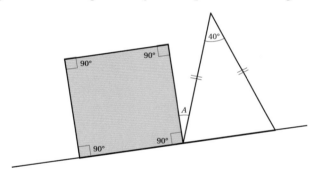

Some of these might not be helpful, but as there are only a few angles on the diagram, you are already narrowing down the problem.

Another piece of information you have got is that the triangle is isosceles. That means you can work out the other angles in the triangle. One angle is given as 40° and you know that all the angles in the triangle add up to 180°. This means the other two add up to 140° and because they are both equal they must each be 70°.

Now mark those angles on the diagram.

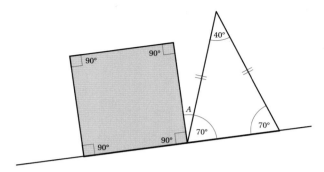

Now you can see what to do!

In the middle of the diagram there are three angles on a straight line. You know that these add up to 180° and you know what two of them are, so you can work out what angle A is.

$90° + 70° = 160°$

$180° − 160° = 20°$

So angle $A = 20°$

Now go back to the question.

In this diagram a square and an isosceles triangle sit on a straight line. Work out the size of angle A.

Check whether you missed out any important information. In this case, you will see that you have used all the information provided in the question.

In this diagram a square (*you used the fact that angles in a square are 90°*) **and an isosceles triangle** (*you used the facts that base angles in an isosceles triangle are equal and that angles in a triangle add up to 180°*) **sit on a straight line** (*you used the fact that angles on a straight line add up to 180°*). **Work out the size of angle A.** (*You've done that*).

The key points are: draw a good diagram, work out the things you can and then write this new information on the diagram.

Here is another example.

> This diagram consists of a square with four semicircles drawn inside. What fraction of the square is shaded?

Don't worry that you can't work out the answer immediately. How about working out the area of the semicircles?

Tip

Remember: Angles on a straight line add up to 180°.

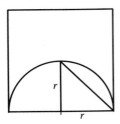

There aren't any measurements, so you could call the radius of the circle r. The area of the semicircle is $\frac{1}{2}\pi r^2$.

If you remove the triangle in the illustration above you get something that is part of the shaded diagram. The area of the triangle is r^2.

Hold on: The shaded parts of this diagram together make one of the 'petals' in the original diagram! One petal has an area of $\frac{1}{2}\pi r^2 - r^2$.

The fraction of the original diagram (which is a square of side $2r$) that is

shaded is $\dfrac{4\left(\frac{1}{2}\pi r^2 - r^2\right)}{(2r)^2}$

The numerator can be factorised to give $\dfrac{4r^2\left(\frac{1}{2}\pi - 1\right)}{4r^2}$ which is $\frac{1}{2}\pi - 1$.

You can check this is sensible by ensuring it is between 0 and 1.

$\frac{1}{2}\pi - 1 \approx 0.57$

The following problems may be solved using more than one method; however, the worked solutions provided at the back of this book are based on the method introduced above.

 Without using a calculator, decide if the statement below is true or false.

$10\sqrt{70} < 80$

Explain your answer.

The maximum safe load of Johnny's van is 840 kg, correct to the nearest 10 kg.

Johnny is going to transport large stone slabs for his next garden project.

The slabs weigh 16 kg each.

Johnny doesn't want to risk damaging his van.

What is the maximum number of slabs Johnny can safely transport in one go in his van?

a Find a formula in terms of x for the area of the shape shown below.

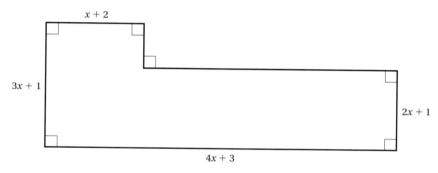

The actual length of the side labelled $3x + 1$ is 16 m.

b Solve the equation $3x + 1 = 16$.

c What is the area of the shape? Give your answer in square metres.

The shape is the plan of a field. Farmer Smith wants to put a fence around the field.

He intends to put three lengths of wire between wooden posts around the field, as shown in the diagram.

wooden posts

wire

Farmer Smith will fix the wooden posts one metre apart.

d How many wooden posts will Farmer Smith need in total?

e What length of wire will Farmer Smith require for three lengths, as shown in the diagram?

Posts cost £18.50 each and wire is sold at £2.30 per metre.

f How much is it going to cost Farmer Smith to fence the field?

Benevolence paid £2.90 for three mangoes and two pawpaw fruits at the market.

Cecilia paid £5.50 for five mangoes and four pawpaw fruits at the same market on Sunday.

What is the price of a mango and the price of a pawpaw fruit?

Sandra wants to make a triangular prism.

She draws the diagram below, cuts it out, folds it up and tapes it together.

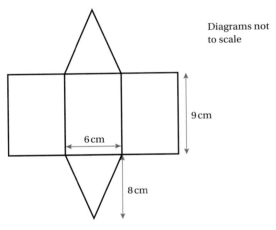

Diagrams not to scale

9 cm

6 cm

8 cm

a What is the volume of the triangular prism?

Chris makes a different prism.

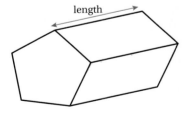

length

The pentagonal faces each have an area of 36 cm².

The volume of Chris's prism is the same as the volume of Sandra's prism.

b Calculate the length of this prism.

Jeff takes a full 500 ml bottle of water and pours himself a drink into the glass shown below. He fills the glass to 2 cm below the top. How much water is left in the bottle?

Diagram not to scale

13 cm

6 cm

Mrs Jones and Miss Smith are writing topic tests for GCSE Mathematics.

Each topic test is going to have 32 questions split in the ratio of 3 : 5 for non-calculator to calculator questions.

a How many non-calculator questions will each topic test contain?

There will eventually be 15 topic tests.

b How many calculator questions in total must be written?

Miss Smith is writing all the non-calculator questions for the 15 tests and some of the calculator questions so that she and Mrs Jones are each writing the same number of questions.

c What fraction of the total questions written by Miss Smith will be calculator questions?

A bag contains green, yellow and white balls. The probability of picking a green ball out of the bag is 0.64. The probability of picking a white ball is the same as the probability of picking a yellow ball.

a What is the probability of picking out a white ball?

b If there are nine yellow balls, what is the number of balls in the bag?

Sharon, Sue, Frances and Anisha are running in a 5 km sponsored race.

The probability of each finishing first out of the four is shown in the table below:

Sharon	0.23
Sue	0.46
Frances	0.15
Anisha	x

What is the probability that either Sue or Anisha finishes first?

The teacher has a dice but doesn't know whether it is biased.
20 students each throw the dice ten times. The number of times each student rolls a six is shown below.

Is the dice biased? Explain your ideas.

Student	Number of sixes in 10 rolls
A	7
B	4
C	3
D	6
E	4
F	3
G	4
H	5
I	5
J	3
K	4
L	5
M	6
N	4
O	5
P	7
Q	0
R	3
S	3
T	2

The mean of five numbers is 12. The numbers are in the ratio
1 : 1 : 3 : 4 : 6.

Find the largest number.

 $\frac{4}{5}$ of the rectangle on the right is shaded.

40 units

30 units

a How many extra square units must be shaded in order to increase
this fraction to $\frac{5}{6}$?

The $\frac{4}{5}$ shaded rectangle is put next to a congruent rectangle that is
$\frac{2}{3}$ shaded.

40 units

30 units

b What fraction of the resulting large rectangle is shaded?

c How many square units need to be shaded to increase the fraction
so that exactly $\frac{3}{4}$ of the large rectangle is shaded?

 Tip

You could draw a diagram showing
the shading in a 'neater' way.

Your younger brother uses his calculator to work out 6 ÷ 0.5 and is
surprised that he gets such a big answer. He tries 6 ÷ 0 and doesn't
understand why it won't tell him the answer.

How could you explain the answers to your brother?

 Tip

Think about how you might do this
in a way that someone younger
than you would understand.
Remember, you have to be clear
enough to change their mind!

An average-sized toilet paper roll is 10.5 cm wide and has a diameter of
12 cm. The hole in the centre has a diameter of 5 cm.

A good-quality paper has a thickness of 0.5 mm and each sheet is 10 cm
long.

Happy Wipes advertise their toilet rolls as the best on the market, with
each roll containing at least 200 good-quality sheets.

Is their claim true?

 Tip

What can you work out? Can you
find the volume of a sheet of toilet
paper? What about the volume of
the toilet roll?

15

The area of the rectangle is the same as the area of the square.

$x + 11$

$x + 1$

$x + 5$

$x + 5$

Diagrams not to scale

How many centimetre squares are needed to cover the rectangle?

 16

A shape is formed by cutting a square from the corner of a larger square, as shown in the diagram below.

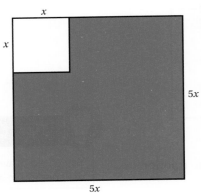

x

x

$5x$

$5x$

Diagram not to scale

a Write an expression for the blue area.

b If the area of the blue shape is 1944 cm^2, find the perimeter of the blue shape.

Alison is planning to make a patchwork quilt for her niece. She has decided to include the flower pattern shown below as part of her design. The centre piece of this flower is a regular hexagon.

Tip

What do you know about a regular hexagon? What angles can you work out? What about a regular pentagon?

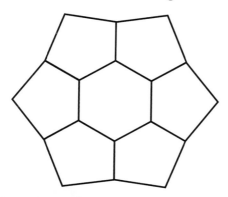

a Show that Alison cannot produce this pattern by using regular pentagons.

b She still wants to use a regular hexagon for the centre piece. Are there any regular polygons that she could put around the edge to form the petals?

c If she wanted to use regular pentagons for the petals, which regular polygon would she need in the centre?

Jenny makes a kite. She starts from a square piece of paper, like this.

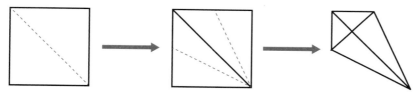

Jenny makes more kites and puts them together around a point. The start of this pattern is shown in the diagram. How many kites does she need altogether so they fit together without any gaps?

In the diagram, *AC* is a diameter of the circle and *AD* = *BC*.

Tip

What do you know about the triangles? Consider how knowing about congruent triangles might help you with this question.

Show that quadrilateral *ABCD* is a rectangle.

A trapezium is inscribed in a circle with centre *O*. ∠*BOC* is 50° and ∠*AOB* is 75°.

a Calculate the size of ∠*COD*.

b What does this tell you about trapezium *ABCD*?

Diagram not to scale

Tip

Draw a clear diagram and write on it the information you are given.
- What is special about the angles?
- What other angles can you calculate?

Tip

What are the properties of a trapezium? How could you use these to help you to answer this question?

Harriet says: 'I think tan *θ* is equal to sin *θ* ÷ cos *θ*.'

Using the values in the table below to justify your response, decide whether Harriet is correct.

θ	$\sin \theta$	$\cos \theta$	$\tan \theta$
0°	0	1	
30°	$\frac{1}{2}$	$\frac{\sqrt{3}}{2}$	
45°	$\frac{\sqrt{2}}{2}$	$\frac{\sqrt{2}}{2}$	
60°	$\frac{\sqrt{3}}{2}$	$\frac{1}{2}$	
90°	1	0	

Sunil has kept woodlice as his pets for a year. They have survived well in their plastic habitat, but the woodlice expert at the pet shop told him he should only keep approximately 150 woodlice in a habitat of that size. Sunil thinks it is getting close to the time when he should let some go free, so he decides to count them by using a capture-mark-release counting method.

He catches 16 woodlice and marks each one with a dot. He then places them back in their habitat. Two days later Sunil catches 16 of his woodlice again and discovers he has recaptured two with the dots.

Using this information, does he need to set any free?

Tip

You can't immediately solve the problem, but you do know what fraction of woodlice have a dot: $\frac{2}{16}$ ($= \frac{1}{8}$). So each time Sunil catches 16 woodlice, he gets about $\frac{1}{8}$ of all the woodlice.

Jo creates a quadrilateral by folding a rectangular piece of paper as shown in the diagram below.

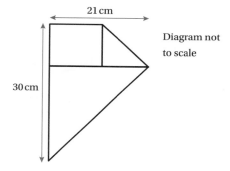

21 cm

30 cm

Diagram not to scale

a What is the area of the quadrilateral?

b What fraction of the original rectangle does the quadrilateral represent?

Tip

For part **b** you could give your answer as a fraction, decimal or percentage. If you choose to use a fraction, make sure you give it in its simplest form.

Mary wants to make a medieval-style hat for her Halloween ball. She will buy a sheet of black card, big enough for her to be able to make the hat without joining any pieces of card together.

The hat must be made from one piece of card.

The hat will be conical in shape with a radius of 9 cm and slant height of 36 cm.

What size of card must Mary buy?

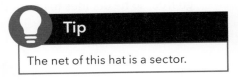

Tip

The net of this hat is a sector.

Tomato soup contains 59 kcalories per 100 ml. Martin is on a diet and has been advised to use a smaller bowl to help reduce his portion sizes. The images on the right show Martin's original bowl and the smaller bowl he will now use. Martin always fills his bowl as close to the brim as possible.

Assuming the two bowls are perfect hemispheres, how many kcalories will he save by eating tomato soup from the smaller bowl? Give your answer to the nearest kcalorie.

Five equilateral triangles are drawn on the edges of a regular pentagon.

Show that polygon created by joining points *F*, *G*, *H*, *I* and *J* is also a regular pentagon.

Many astronomical distances are measured in light years. A light year is the distance that light travels in a vacuum in one year.

Light travels at approximately 2.99×10^5 km/s.

The distance to Proxima Centuri is approximately 4.22 light years.

How many laps of a standard 400 m running track is this equivalent to?

> **Tip**
>
> What can you work out? How far does light travel in a minute/hour/year?

Look at the two triangles drawn on this coordinate grid.

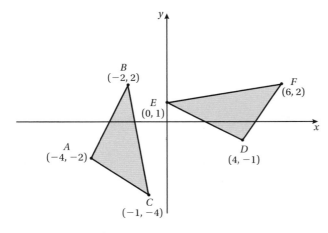

Show that the two triangles are congruent.

> **Tip**
>
> You can't say straightaway if they are congruent, but you can calculate the lengths of some sides.
>
> Remember to refer to the conditions for congruence.

The hare and the tortoise are having a race. The hare is confident and offers the tortoise a shortcut across the middle of the rectangular field.

If the tortoise totters along at 0.1 m/s, what is the lowest speed the hare could run at and still win the race?

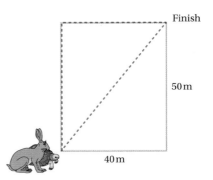

Adding lines is a strategy that works for some geometry problems. Sometimes an extra line is very helpful. On other occasions it turns out to be useless. How can you tell which type of line to use? Let's work through an example problem.

> In the diagram below, two parallel lines are shown. Work out the size of angle α.

There are several different ways to solve this problem. Here are three of them, all of which involve adding extra lines to the diagram.

Solution 1

Add a line parallel to the other two lines that passes through the angle you want to work out:

Could this help you?

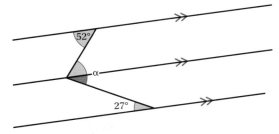

The angle shown in red is equal to 27°. Can you explain why?

What is the other part of angle α equal to? What is angle α?

Solution 2

Add a line that is perpendicular to the parallel lines and passes through the point of the angle, as shown in the next diagram.

You now have two triangles. In those triangles you know two of the angles, so you can work out the third one. Do that now, remembering to mark the angles on the diagram. Here you are making use of the strategy from Chapter 2 and advice from Chapter 1 to annotate a diagram by adding new information when you work it out.

In the middle of this diagram there is a straight line, so now you can work out the missing angle α.

Solution 3

Add a line that is perpendicular to the parallel lines and passes through the point of the 27° angle as shown in the diagram below.

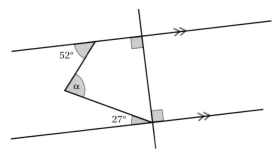

You can see a quadrilateral in the middle of the diagram. You can also 'see' what to do to solve the problem, because you can work out three of the angles in the quadrilateral and you know that all of the angles add up to 360°.

Let's go back to the question we posed at the beginning: How can you tell which type of line to use?

The short answer is that you can't. There are lots of different lines you could have drawn on this diagram that wouldn't have helped you. For example, the line in the next diagram doesn't do anything special and is not helpful.

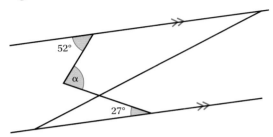

A line that is 'special' in some way is more likely to be helpful.

Try using lines that:

- are parallel to other lines
- are perpendicular to other lines
- are lines of symmetry
- join up two points
- are midpoints of sides of shapes.

The following problems may be solved using more than one method; however, the worked solutions provided at the back of this book are based on the method introduced above.

> **Tip**
>
> You may need to try out several ideas before one works!

Students taking part in a mathematical challenge are shown the image below.

They are asked: 'What proportion of the outer triangle is coloured purple?'

After some thought, the teams hand in their answers.

Team **A**: 24 cm^2

Team **B**: $\frac{3}{4}$

Team **C**: $(\frac{3}{4})^2$

Team **D**: 0.5625

How many marks out of four would you award each team?

Justify your decisions.

Gerry has a swimming pool at his holiday home. He needs to put a short fence around the pool to prevent small children falling in.

He wants the fence to surround the pool completely, at a distance of 1 m from the edge.

a Calculate the length of fencing that Gerry will need to buy. Give your answer correct to three significant figures.

Ian also needs to build a fence around his pool, but it is a different shape from Gerry's. Ian would like to build his fence 1.5 m from the edge of the pool.

b Will Ian need to buy more fencing than Gerry? Explain your answer.

The perimeter of the shape shown on the right is 2.28 km.

Calculate the value of a. Give your answer in kilometres.

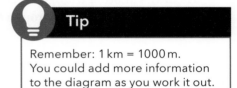

> **Tip**
>
> Remember: 1 km = 1000 m.
> You could add more information to the diagram as you work it out.

Robyn is designing a template for an art project. She plans to cut a regular octagon in half through two vertices and place them side by side, as shown below (the base is a straight line).

Robyn is trying to calculate the size of the angle labelled a.

Show two ways in which Robyn could do this.

Mandeep is investigating patterns in circles. He draws eight dots equally spaced around a circle.

He draws a triangle by connecting three of the dots. The line *AC* passes through the centre of the circle, *O*.

Diagrams not to scale

Tip

Drawing extra lines on the diagrams can help you to answer questions like this. Think carefully which line to draw.

a Use this image to show that ∠*ABC* is a right angle.

He draws another triangle by connecting a different set of three dots. The line *AC* still passes through the centre of the circle.

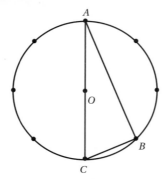

b Is ∠*ABC* a right angle?

Mandeep draws a different circle and marks ten dots equally spaced around its circumference. Once again, he draws a triangle by connecting three of these dots. The line *AC* passes through the centre of the circle.

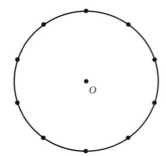

c Show that for a triangle of your choice that meets these conditions, the sum of ∠*BAC* and ∠*BCA* is 90°.

A circle is inscribed in a triangle as shown below. What is the value of *x*?

Diagram not to scale

Tip

Join the centre of the circle to the three points of contact with the tangents.

Show how the shape below could be divided into:

a three congruent shapes

b four congruent shapes.

Tip

Make several copies of the diagram and try out your ideas.

Charlie's house has two floors connected by a staircase. The vertical distance between the two floors is 3.6 m. Each step in the staircase is 18 cm high and 28 cm deep.

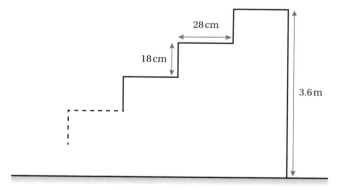

a How many steps are there in the staircase?

b How long will the banister rail be?

35

A rectangular tabletop has a perimeter of 12 m. The width of the table is x m.

a Write an expression in terms of x for the surface area of the tabletop.

The area of the tabletop is 6.3 m².

b Would a tablecloth measuring 2.2 m by 3.1 m fit cover this tabletop?

The graphs of two quadratic equations are shown below.

The blue parabola is symmetrical about the line $x = 2$ and has roots at A and B.

The blue parabola is reflected in the x-axis to create the red parabola. The red parabola has roots at C and D.

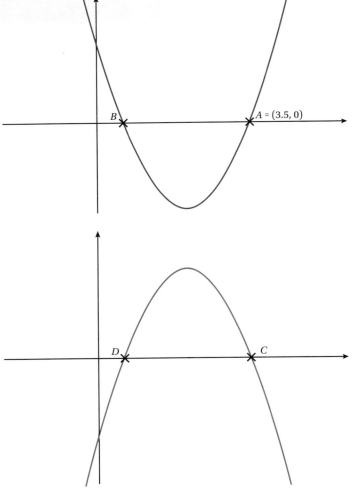

Work out the coordinates of points B, C and D.

Liz looks up at the clock on her office wall. She is disappointed to see that it is not yet five o'clock, time to go home.

Tip

Remember that on an analogue clock, the hour hand and the minute hand both move continuously. What angle does each hand turn through in one hour?

a Through how many degrees must the clock's minute hand turn before Liz can leave work?

b Through what angle must the hour hand turn before Liz can leave?

As shown in the diagram below:

$\overrightarrow{SW} = 3\mathbf{v}$, $\overrightarrow{ST} = 2\mathbf{u}$

$\overrightarrow{SR} = -\frac{1}{2}\mathbf{u}$, $\overrightarrow{SX} = -2\mathbf{v}$

$\overrightarrow{SP}$ is the diagonal of parallelogram $SWPT$ and $\overrightarrow{SZ}$ is the diagonal of parallelogram $SRZX$.

Tip

Drawing a clear diagram will help you see what is happening here.

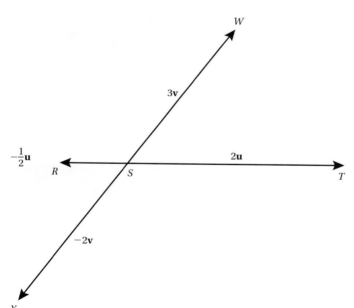

Are Z, S and P colinear?

13

A giant paperclip is placed against a ruler as shown below. The curved ends are semicircles.

Diagram not to scale

a Calculate the length of wire needed to make this paperclip. Give your answer correct to one decimal place.

A second paperclip is placed against the ruler.

b Which paperclip uses the greater length of wire?

Tip

You may need to use Pythagoras' theorem in this question.

14

In an isosceles triangle the lengths of the sides are $(2x - 1)$ cm and $(2x - 4)$ cm.

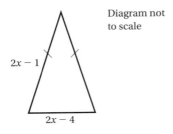

Diagram not to scale

$2x - 1$

$2x - 4$

Tip

Which topic will help you to work out the height?

a Work out the algebraic expression for the perpendicular height of this triangle.

b If the perpendicular height of the triangle is 12 cm, find the area of the triangle.

Students on a field trip are told that they can use a clever trick to estimate the height of a tall tree. They are told to point their arm at an angle of approximately 45° and to look along it. They then walk backwards until their arm is pointing to the top of the tree.

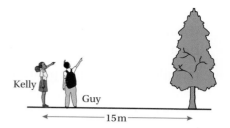

The distance from the student to the tree trunk is approximately the same as the height of the tree, plus the student's own height.

a Explain why this method gives a rough answer.

Two students, Kelly and Guy, try this out. Guy ends up standing 3 m in front of Kelly.

b If Kelly's angle is exactly 45°, at what angle must Guy be holding his arm?

Lorna is going to Glasgow for a fortnight. She is travelling from London. There are a couple of different options for getting to Glasgow.

Lorna can go by coach, which travels direct from London to Glasgow. Alternatively, she can go by train with a change in Birmingham and a wait of 1 hour 45 minutes.

The distance from London to Glasgow is 650 km.

The coach leaves at 06.30 and takes exactly eight hours to arrive in Glasgow.

If Lorna goes by train, she would leave London at 07.00 and arrive in Birmingham at 08.00.

The train journey from Birmingham to Glasgow should then take 4 hours 15 minutes.

a What is the average speed for the coach journey?

b What is the average speed for the train journey?

17

Six cylindrical candles are held together in a plastic sleeve in the formation shown on the right. Each candle has a radius of 2.7 cm.

Calculate the length of plastic needed to hold the candles tightly. Give your answer correct to two decimal places.

Tip

Think about the plastic being wrapped around just one candle. What about two candles?

18

ABCDEF is a regular hexagon.

A has coordinates (2, 1).

The column vector for $\overrightarrow{AB} = \begin{pmatrix} 0 \\ 2 \end{pmatrix}$

a What is the column vector for $\overrightarrow{DE}$?

b Find the coordinates of *C*.

c What is the column vector for $\overrightarrow{BC}$?

d What is the column vector for $\overrightarrow{FC}$?

e What is the column vector for $\overrightarrow{AE}$?

f What is the column vector for $\overrightarrow{AC}$?

g What is the column vector for $\overrightarrow{EF}$?

Tip

Some of your answers will involve surds.

19

The circle has a radius of 5 and is centred on the origin. The point (3, 4) lies on the circle.

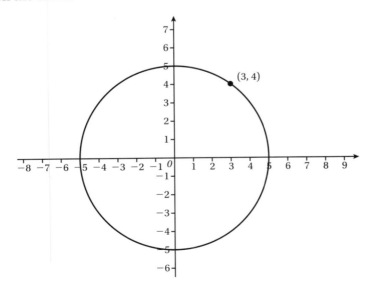

a Find the equation of the tangent to the circle at this point.

b Use your answer to part **a** to write down the equation of another tangent to the circle.

Two straight lines are drawn from a point *A* outside a circle to two points, *B* and *C*, on the circumference of the circle. The lengths of the four arcs created are marked in the diagram in terms of *x*.

Calculate the size of $\angle BAC$.

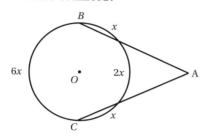

Diagram not to scale

Tip

Are there any useful lines that you can draw to make this problem look more 'friendly'?
Why have you been told the arc lengths? What does this have to do with angles in the circle?

  Two triangles are shown below.

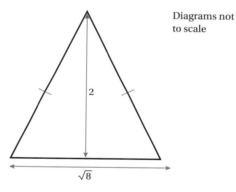

Diagrams not to scale

Triangle **A**   Triangle **B**

Without using a calculator, explain which triangle has:

a the greater perimeter   **b** the greater area.

A square is inscribed inside a circle with a 1 cm radius as shown below.

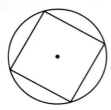

a Calculate the area of the square.

An equilateral triangle is inscribed in a circle.

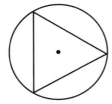

b Show that the ratio of the area of the triangle to the area of the square in part **a**, is approximately $2 : 3$.

A regular pentagon is inscribed in a circle.

c Show that the area of the pentagon is approximately $\frac{6}{5}$ the area of the square in part **a**.

Sometimes there is a problem that is just too complicated to solve immediately. One way to deal with this is to make the problem simpler. This won't directly tell you the answer because it will be a slightly different problem, but it might give you a starting point that will help you get to the answer. Here's an example.

> George climbs a staircase that has ten steps. He can go from one step to the next one (1-step), or can miss out a step and go up two at once (2-step). How many different ways can he go up the ten steps?

You could start by drawing a diagram, but you will quickly produce a picture that has too many lines on it, like the one on the right.

You could also start to write down the different possibilities, using 1 to stand for '1-step' and 2 to stand for '2-step'.

So:

1111111111

1211212

22222

and so on.

But there are too many possibilities and it just looks too hard.

You could make the problem simpler. Let's make it very simple indeed. Imagine that George wants to climb a staircase with one step.

This is easy: one way (if he tries to do a 2-step he will only actually go up one step). Now try two steps. There are two ways. The diagram on the right shows the working.

You could now look at the pattern of answers to see if that will help, as shown in the table below.

Number of steps	Number of ways of climbing them
1	1
2	2
3	3
4	5
5	8

Do you recognise the number sequence in the second column?

1, 2, 3, 5, 8 is part of the Fibonacci Sequence, where you add the two previous numbers to get the next one. 1 + 2 = 3, 2 + 3 = 5, 3 + 5 = 8. If this is the right sequence then the next one will be 5 + 8 = 13. You don't want to draw this out, so instead think about why this might be sensible.

When you look at the numbers written next to each flight of stairs you can see some similarities.

Here are the routes up five steps:	**If you remove the final number you get this sequence:**	
11111	1111	← **and these are the ways of climbing three and four steps!**
2111	211	
221	22	
212	21	
1211	121	
122	12	
1112	111	
1121	112	

Why does that make sense?

Well, if you want to climb five steps, you could go up four steps and then do a 1-step to get to the top. So you need all of the ways of climbing four steps with a 1 at the end. Alternatively, you can get to three steps and then do a 2-step to get to the top, so you need all of the ways of climbing three steps with a 2 after them. This means you really are adding the previous two numbers together.

To climb ten steps you need to continue the sequence: 1, 2, 3, 5, 8, 13, 21, 34, 55, 89. So there are 89 ways to climb the ten stairs.

Here, simplifying the problem meant you could get started and could see what was going on.

Let's look at another example problem.

> What is the smallest number that can be divided (with no remainder) by all numbers from 1 to 20?

What do you know already?

Clearly the number will have to end with a zero (to make it divisible by 10). It will have to be even so it is divisible by 2 (but if it ends with a zero then that is already the case).

One strategy that might be useful is to make the problem simpler.

Change the problem so it now says this:

What is the smallest number that can be divided by all numbers from 1 to 3?

If you do $2 \times 3 = 6$ then you know that 6 can be divided by 1, 2 and 3. Is it the smallest number? Yes.

Another change:

What is the smallest number that can be divided by all numbers from 1 to 4?

If you do $2 \times 3 \times 4 = 24$ then you know that can be divided by 1, 2, 3 and 4. But there is a smaller number that works. 12 can be divided by 1, 2, 3 and 4. Why didn't $2 \times 3 \times 4$ give you the right answer? To make it divisible by 4 you didn't need to multiply the previous answer by 4, because there was already a 2 involved. If you had just multiplied that previous answer by 2 that would have given you a number divisible by 4.

Therefore the answer is $2 \times 3 \times 2 = 12$.

Do you notice that these numbers are prime numbers?

Try the next one:

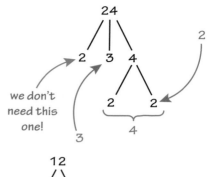

we don't need this one!

What is the smallest number that can be divided by all numbers from 1 to 5?

You currently have $2 \times 3 \times 2$, which is not helpful if you want it to be divisible by 5. The trick that you used with 4 (splitting it into 2×2) won't work here because 5 is a prime number. To make it a multiple of 5 you will need to multiply by 5, giving you $2 \times 3 \times 2 \times 5 = 60$.

You can see that the next one is easy.

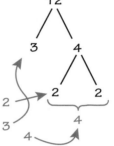

What is the smallest number that can be divided by all numbers from 1 to 6?

60 is obviously already divisible by 6, and you can see that in the numbers because 2×3 is in there. $2 \times 3 \times 2 \times 5$ is divisible by all numbers from 1 to 6.

To make the smallest number divisible by 7 we need to include a 7, because you cannot make 7 by multiplying smaller numbers (7 is a prime number).

To make it divisible by 7 you therefore need to have $2 \times 3 \times 2 \times 5 \times 7$.

To make it divisible by 8 you only need an extra 2 because your number is already divisible by 4, and to make it divisible by 9 you need an extra 3.

Then this is already divisible by 10.

Now you can finish off the problem by thinking about each of the numbers from 11 up to 20 as shown in the table below.

11	Needed, prime number	**16**	Have 8, so just need extra 2
12	Have already ($2 \times 2 \times 3$)	**17**	Needed, prime number
13	Needed, prime number	**18**	Have already ($2 \times 3 \times 3$)
14	Have already (2×7)	**19**	Needed, prime number
15	Have already (3×5)	**20**	Have already ($2 \times 2 \times 5$)

Your final answer is therefore:

$2 \times 2 \times 2 \times 3 \times 3 \times 5 \times 7 \times 11 \times 13 \times 17 \times 19 = 232\,792\,560$

The following problems may be solved using more than one method; however, the worked solutions provided at the back of this book are based on the method introduced above.

Anna knows that she can create a heart shape from a triangle and two semicircles. She makes a Valentine's card by cutting a heart shape out of a rectangle of red cardboard 9 cm by 13 cm, as shown below.

What area of red cardboard has Anna removed from the original piece to make her card? Give your answer correct to three significant figures.

Ahmed buys a piece of wood measuring 12 cm by 5 cm by 1 m for £5.

He uses the wood to make door wedges like this.

Diagram not to scale

a He made 40 wedges from the piece of wood he bought. What is the width x cm of these wedges?

b What is the lowest price Ahmed could sell the wedges for to make at least £30 profit?

Larry's aunt gives him £40 000 to put into a compound interest savings account.

ABC Bank is offering 8% compound interest if you invest more than £30 000 and the money remains in the bank for at least ten years.

Larry's aunt tells him that his money will more than double if he invests his money for ten years.

a Is Larry's aunt correct?

b What is the exact amount Larry will have in his account at the end of ten years?

Larry's aunt decides to invest some of her own money for ten years. She wants to make a profit and have a total of at least £75 000 at the end of the ten-year period.

c What is the smallest amount (to the nearest £1000) she must invest to have at least £75 000 at the end of ten years?

Is it possible for you to count from one to a million in your lifetime?

> **Tip**
>
> Don't try this out! What easier version of this question could you try out? There isn't an exact counting speed, so you won't get an exact answer!

Consider each of the calculations below. Without using a calculator decide whether the answer is odd or even. Explain your reasoning.

a $4^3 + 3^4$ 　　　　　　　　　　**b** $6^7 + 3^7$

Helen drives to work every day. On her journey there is a level crossing, a set of traffic lights and a roundabout. At each of these she must either stop or is allowed to continue.

STOP
when
lights show

The probability of stopping at the level crossing is $\frac{1}{10}$.

The probability of stopping at the lights is $\frac{1}{4}$.

The probability of stopping at the roundabout is $\frac{2}{3}$.

What is the probability that on Helen's next journey to work she has to stop at least once?

Hamish loves to go eagle-spotting in the Scottish Highlands.

If he wakes up early and is able to be in the Cairngorms National Park before 7 am, the probability of him seeing a golden eagle is 0.7. If Hamish wakes up late and does not arrive until after 7 am, his chance of spotting a golden eagle is 0.4.

The probability of Hamish waking up early on the morning of one of his planned trips is 0.85.

a What is the probability that, on a day picked at random, Hamish will see a golden eagle on one of his trips?

Sometimes Hamish takes his younger sister, Elspeth, with him.

The probability of Elspeth waking up early enough to allow them to arrive before 7 am is 0.75.

b What is the probability that Hamish will **not** see a golden eagle when his sister is on the trip with him?

c What happens to Hamish's chances of seeing a golden eagle if Elspeth goes with him?

Two almost identical logos are shown below. Both show a square of side length 10 cm with a second square tilted inside it.

a Do they have the same total line length?

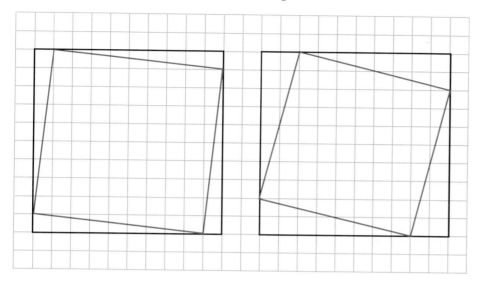

A third logo is created in the same style. The tilted square in this logo has an area exactly half that of the original tilted square.

b Make an accurate drawing of this logo on squared paper.

Dave is travelling 280 km from Milton Keynes to Weymouth. He is travelling by car and a graph of his journey is shown here.

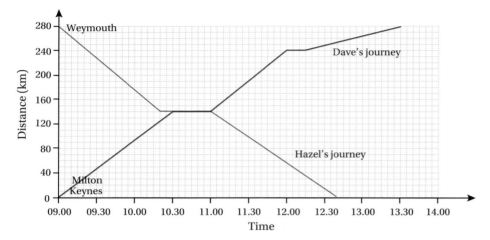

Hazel is travelling from Weymouth to Milton Keynes on the same day as Dave, but on a motorcycle.

A graph of Hazel's journey is also shown.

Both Dave and Hazel set out on their journeys at 09.00.

a What was Dave's speed for the first 140 km?

b What was Hazel's speed for the first stage of her journey?

c How long did Hazel have to wait before Dave arrived at the service station where they were meeting for a coffee?

d Dave got caught up in a traffic jam just outside of Weymouth. At what time was this?

e How long did Dave's journey take? What was his average speed?

f How long did Hazel's journey take? What was her average speed?

Who is the oldest?

Shirley — 14.2 years

Ross — 169 months

Jemima — 5293 days

Dave — 450 million seconds

The area of rectangle **A** is the same as the area of rectangle **B**.

Find the value of a.

Diagrams not to scale

a

$\sqrt{2}$ **A**

B $\sqrt{10}$

$2\sqrt{5}$

A small rectangle is cut out of a larger rectangle and thrown away. Calculate the proportion of the original rectangle that is left.

$\sqrt{28}$

Diagram not to scale

$\sqrt{12}$

$\sqrt{3}$

$\sqrt{7}$

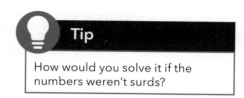

Tip

How would you solve it if the numbers weren't surds?

A garden centre sells two types of hanging basket.

Tip

The right-hand basket is a hemisphere. What is a hemisphere? How would you calculate its volume?

Assuming that both types have the same diameter and that the height of the conical basket is also equal to its diameter, which basket has the greater volume?

Greg is starting a bakery. He wants to advertise nutritional information on his homemade cakes.

He follows this recipe and increases it to make a batch of 30 muffins:

<u>Makes 12</u>

2 eggs   200 g caster sugar   250 ml milk

125 ml vegetable oil   400 g flour   1 tsp salt

1 Egg
Fat: 4.6 g
Sugar: Trace

Milk
Fat: 2%
Sugar: 5%

Vegetable oil
Fat: 100%
Sugar: 0%

Flour
Fat: $\frac{7}{500}$
Sugar: $\frac{1}{1000}$

Greg knows that 1 ml of liquid weighs about 1 g.

a What is the amount, in grams, of sugar and fat in each muffin?

The GDA (guideline daily amount) of fat is 70 g and sugar is 90 g.

b What should Greg advertise as the percentage of the GDA in each of his muffins?

A mug is printed with a chequerboard pattern made up of squares that have been rotated through 45°. Exactly five of these white squares fit around the mug. The diameter of the mug is 9 cm. Calculate the perimeter of one square on the mug.

Give your answer correct to three significant figures.

Tip

Think of the design as a rectangle that has been wrapped around the mug. Draw a diagram to show the net of the cup with the squares on it. How long will the rectangle be?

Making changes to the problem is another strategy that works particularly well with some geometric problems. This time you won't necessarily simplify the problem (like you did in the previous chapter). Instead you could adjust it in a way that doesn't change its important features. This might allow you to see what is going on.

> In the first diagram on the right, AB is the diameter of the circle, C lies on the circumference and O is the centre of the circle. What is the relationship between the area of triangle OAC and triangle OBC? Explain your answer.

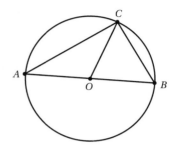

The question asks: 'What is the relationship?' What could that mean? Perhaps one is double the other? Maybe they are the same?

In the first diagram it looks as if the areas might be the same. Can you provide evidence to convince yourself that this is the case?

After that, can you convince someone else that this is the case?

The key points are:

- there is a circle

- AB is the diameter of the circle

- O is the centre of the circle

- points A, B and C are on the circle. All of this must stay true.

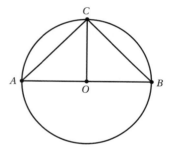

You might be able to move some of the points so the answer is obvious. There doesn't seem to be anything special about the placing of point C, so it might be acceptable for you to move this point around. It wouldn't be acceptable for you to move C off the circle, though, because that would change the situation.

In the second diagram, C has moved so that it is halfway between A and B but still on the circle. There is now a line of symmetry in the diagram and the two triangles are clearly equal.

The third diagram is another special case.

C has moved so that it is on top of point B. This time the two triangles both have zero area, so they are the same.

The idea that the two areas are the same is looking plausible.

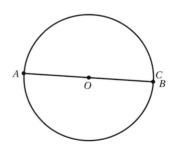

How do you work out the area of a triangle?

It is half of the base multiplied by the perpendicular height.

In the yellow triangle on the right, the area is the radius of the circle (*OB*) multiplied by the dashed line (the perpendicular height), divided by two.

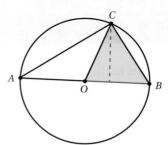

In the purple triangle on the right, the area is the radius of the circle (*AO*) multiplied by the perpendicular height, divided by two. But what is the perpendicular height for the purple triangle? It is actually the dashed line.

So they do have the same area and you can explain why.

This is also an example of where adding an extra line can help us, see Chapter *3 Adding lines*.

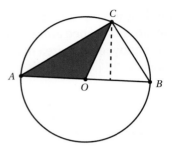

So, what sort of changes might be useful?

- Moving points around (but preserving the initial situation)
- Trying to make a special situation (e.g. a line of symmetry)
- Moving points to extreme positions.

A good diagram is also important here, see Chapter 1 *Draw a diagram*.

The following problems may be solved using more than one method; however, the worked solutions provided at the back of this book are based on the method introduced above.

 Alina is asked to choose five different fractions and write them down in ascending order.

She thinks carefully and then writes:

$$\frac{1}{6} \qquad \frac{1}{5} \qquad \frac{1}{4} \qquad \frac{1}{3} \qquad \frac{1}{2}$$

a Suggest another set of fractions that she could have written.

b Suggest another set of fractions where none has a numerator of 1.

c Suggest another set of fractions with greater numerators than denominators.

Tip

There are lots of ways to do this. One way is to change the original set of fractions.

Which is bigger?

a	400 g + 400 mg	or	0.5 kg − 90 g
b	0.1 km + 150 cm	or	110 m − 900 cm
c	0.75 h + 600 s	or	50 min + 0.1 h

In a restaurant chairs can be arranged around square tables as shown below.

a How many chairs are needed if five tables are arranged in this way?

b Find the rule for the number of chairs needed for n tables.

The restaurant owner has a total of 55 chairs.

c Is it possible to use all 55 chairs with tables arranged like this? Explain your answer.

The restaurant needs to be set up for 32 guests at a function. The party leader wants the guests to be split into two equal groups at two large tables.

d How many small square tables will the owner use to make each of these large table settings?

Elliott has a bag of coloured balls with red, green and yellow balls.

The probability of picking a red ball at random is $\frac{3}{7}$.

The probability of picking a yellow ball at random is the same as picking a green ball.

a There are nine red balls. How many balls are there in total?

Elliot adds more red and yellow balls to the bag. The probability of picking a green ball at random is now $\frac{3}{25}$.

b What is the total number of balls in Elliott's bag now?

On average there are more than 100 000 strands of hair on a child's head. Blondes average about 140 000 strands, brunettes 108 000 strands and redheads 90 000 strands. The average person loses roughly 0.25% of their hair strands each year.

If hair did not grow back:

a Roughly what percentage of their hair strands would redheads lose after 82 years?

b How many years would it take for an average blonde to lose one tenth of their hair strands?

Lucy chooses three consecutive integers and adds them together.

5 + 6 + 7 = 18

She notices that 18 is also the result of 6 × 3.

Lucy selects another set of three numbers and adds them together.

2 + 3 + 4 = 9

She notices that 9 is also the result of 3 × 3.

It looks like the sum of three consecutive numbers is the same as the middle number multiplied by three.

a Is this always true?

b Can you find a rule for adding four consecutive integers?

c How might you extend your rule to add five or more consecutive integers?

23.64 × 805 = 1903.02

How can you tell that this statement is incorrect?

Four snails have a race.

Assuming that the snails move at a constant speed to the finish line, which one will get there first?

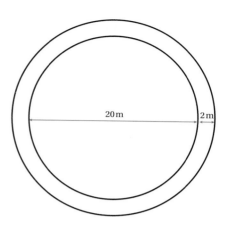

Animals in zoos are normally kept behind double fences to keep them in and the public out.

This style of circular pen is used for the chipmunks and rats. It has a diameter of 20 m. It is surrounded by a double fence with a gap of 2 m between the fences.

a How much longer is the outside fence than the inner fence?

b Suppose the gap was changed to 3 m. What would the difference be then in the length of the fences?

c What is the general rule?

d What happens if the pens are square or rectangular in shape?

The diagram shows two cereal packets.

Tip

There are several steps to this problem. You could start by calculating the volume and surface area of each packet.

Mary says: 'I think the Choc Flakes packet has the greater volume.'

Kelly says: 'I think the Bio Wheat packet has the greater surface area.'

Raymon says: 'Only one of you can be correct. Whichever packet has the greater volume must also have the greater surface area.'

Who is correct? Justify your answer.

Daisy draws a shape on a coordinate grid as shown below:

Tip

Remember to use vector notation to describe a particular translation.
Is there more than one solution to each part of this question? If so, can you write your answers in a more general way (using words or mathematical notation)?

She notices that the centre of her shape (marked with the black dot on the diagram) lies on the line $x = -5$.

a How could you translate her shape so that its centre remains on the line $x = -5$?

Daisy's shape also lies on the line $y = x$.

b How could you translate Daisy's shape so that its centre remains on the line $y = x$?

c How could you translate Daisy's shape so that its centre lies on the line $y = x + 3$?

Melissa has designed this logo for her new business. It is based on an isosceles triangle with a semicircle on each edge.

Calculate the perimeter of Melissa's logo. Give your answer correct to two decimal places.

Diagram not to scale

Tip

Remember:
You can use Pythagoras' theorem to calculate missing lengths in right-angled triangles.

Calculate the mean of the following three numbers:

$$\sqrt{24} \qquad \sqrt{54} \qquad \sqrt{96}$$

Tip

What change will you need to make before you can add the three numbers?

Mikey is asked to investigate what happens when a shape is reflected in two perpendicular mirror lines in turn.

He draws the following picture and makes the observation: 'Ah! The result is the same as a translation of the original shape.'

Tip

'Perpendicular' means that the mirror lines are at right angles (90°) to each other.

Why did Mikey choose his pair of mirror lines to be the x and y axes? Are there other pairs that he could have chosen?

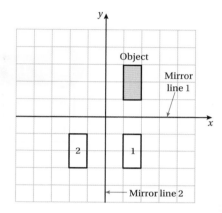

Mikey's teacher looks at his work and asks: 'Are you sure?'

a Suggest what Mikey could do next to investigate this.

b By considering the starting point shown in the diagram below, decide whether or not you agree with Mikey's first idea.

a What is the same and what is different about the following fractions and their decimal equivalents?

$$\frac{1}{9}, \frac{1}{99}, \frac{1}{999}, \frac{1}{9999}, \frac{1}{99999}, \frac{1}{999999}$$

b Explain how you can use your findings to work out the equivalent fraction to each of these recurring decimals. Do this part without a calculator.

 i 0.7777... (repeating 7s)

 ii 5.3333... (repeating 3s)

 iii 0.14444... (repeating 4s)

 iv 2.5000900090009... (repeating 0009s)

Tip

You know about 0.1111... What will 0.2222... be?
How can this help?
Remember to consider the equivalent decimal number to each fraction.

Each of the seven small triangles in the diagram is isosceles. The large outer triangle is also isosceles.

Given one angle, can you work out all the others?

12°   Diagram not to scale

Jessie says: 'No. You don't have enough information.'

Helen says: 'Yes. You can work out all of the other angles.'

Pete says; 'I wonder what would happen to the other angles if the first one was 10° instead of 12°.'

a Decide whether Jessie or Helen is correct. Make sure you justify your answer.

b Try out Pete's idea. What would happen if he started with an angle of 10°?

c Is there a different starting angle for which this **will** work?

Tip

Read the question carefully. What information can you use? Can you label anything on the diagram?

Jack holds out a £1 coin and tries to just cover up the moon. He can't make it fit – the coin is too big. He gets a friend to hold the coin steady and moves backwards until the coin is just a good fit over the moon. He finds that he has had to walk approximately 2.5 m away from the coin.

Given that the moon has a diameter of 3474.8 km, and a £1 coin has a diameter of 22.5 mm, use Jack's findings to estimate the distance of the moon from the Earth.

Tip

Try to draw a diagram showing Jack, the coin and the moon. Label the lengths that you know and the distance that you want to find. Remember to make some conversions!

When you have done a lot of problem solving you might come across problems similar to others you have worked on before. Even if they are not identical you might find that some of the ideas you used in the earlier problem can help you out.

> Multiply two consecutive even numbers. Do you always get a multiple of 8? Justify your answer.

You could start by trying a few to see if it appears to be true (but this won't justify or prove it):

$2 \times 4 = 8$ $6 \times 8 = 48$

$4 \times 6 = 24$ $10 \times 12 = 120$

All of these are multiples of 8. It is looking good so far (but you haven't justified it).

You could approach this problem by looking at factors, but you could also use some algebra.

What can you use for the two numbers? If you call them a and b then that doesn't include the idea that they are **even** numbers. If you call them $2a$ and $2b$ then that could help. You need a and b to be consecutive whole numbers. This tells us that either a or b is even. If you do $2a \times 2b$ you get $4ab$, but since one of a and b is even the whole thing must be a multiple of 8.

Here is a slightly more formal way to do the same thing, using just a single letter. If the first even number is $2a$ then you can call the next one $2a + 2$. When you multiply these you get $2a(2a + 2)$. This is equal to $4a^2 + 4a$, which is $4a(a + 1)$.

Let's look at $4a(a + 1)$.

If a is odd then $a + 1$ is even and we have $4 \times$ odd $\times$ even, which is a multiple of 8 (because 4 multiplied by an even number is a multiple of 8). If $a + 1$ is odd then a is even and we have $4 \times$ even $\times$ odd, which is a multiple of 8.

So the whole thing is a multiple of 8.

> Choose any three consecutive positive integers. Add them together. Is the answer always a multiple of 3? Is the answer always a multiple of 6? Explain your answer.

This problem is similar to the previous one, so you could use some similar techniques.

First, try a few numbers just to get a feel for what is going on. Then use some algebra and try to create an expression to describe what is happening.

$1 + 2 + 3 = 6$ This is a multiple of 3 and also a multiple of 6.

$2 + 3 + 4 = 9$ This is a multiple of 3 but is not a multiple of 6.

You have already shown that the answer is **not** always a multiple of 6 because you have found one that doesn't work.

Using algebra, you could call the first number a. The next number will therefore be $a + 1$ and the one after that will be $a + 2$. This is similar to what you did in the previous example so you are using the experience you gained doing that question.

When you add these together you get $a + a + 1 + a + 2$, which equals $3a + 3$. To show that this is clearly divisible by 3 you could factorise: $3(a + 1)$, to show that you have an integer $(a + 1)$ multiplied by 3.

If you call the middle number n then it happens to be even easier. The three numbers are: $n - 1$, n, $n + 1$, and adding these gives $3n$. Note that you didn't use three different letters to describe the numbers. This is often useful.

You can use some similar techniques to help you work on this next problem.

> Think of a number (a positive integer), square it and subtract the original number. When is the answer a prime number? Explain your answer.

$$1^2 - 1 = 0 \qquad\qquad 3^2 - 3 = 6 \qquad\qquad 5^2 - 5 = 20$$

$$2^2 - 2 = 2 \qquad\qquad 4^2 - 4 = 12 \qquad\qquad 6^2 - 6 = 30$$

So far this looks interesting. You always seem to get an even number as the answer. Does that seem sensible? Will that ever change?

Only one of the answers is a prime number: $2^2 - 2 = 2$.

There are several ways you could continue here, but one is to use some algebra like you did in Examples 1 and 2.

Call the number you thought of n. Then you get $n^2 - n$.

This can be factorised to give $n(n - 1)$. But a prime number has exactly two factors, so if this is going to be prime then one of the numbers n and $n - 1$ has to be equal to 1.

If $n = 1$ then you get $1^2 - 1 = 0$, which doesn't work (because 0 is not a prime number).

If $n - 1 = 1$ then $n = 2$ and you get the answer you know about already: $2^2 - 2 = 2$.

All the others will have extra factors, so they cannot be prime numbers.

For example: $7^2 - 7 = 7 \times 6$.

This means the only prime number you get is 2.

The following problems may be solved using more than one method; however, the worked solutions provided at the back of this book are based on the method introduced above.

Prices for laying lawns are directly proportional to the area of the lawn.

For a lawn measuring 8 m by 10 m, there is a charge of £320.

For a lawn measuring 12 m by 12 m, there is a charge of £576.

a How much will it cost to lay a lawn measuring 12 m by 8 m?

b A lawn costs £560. If the measurements are in metres, what dimensions could the lawn be?

Cooking times for poultry are 50 minutes per kilogram, plus an additional 30 minutes.

For Christmas lunch, Fergus needs to cook a 3 kg chicken and a 7.5 kg turkey.

He wants both birds to be ready at the same time. Fergus needs 20 minutes to carve and prepare the serving dishes, once they are taken out of the oven. He wants to serve lunch at 1.00 pm on Christmas Day.

a How long will the turkey be in the oven by itself before being joined by the chicken?

b Find a formula to find the time taken, t minutes, to cook a chicken weighing m kg.

For New Year's Day Fergus plans to cook a goose. This goose will take 5 hours 5 minutes to cook.

c How much does the goose weigh?

d If Fergus plans to have a late lunch at 2.30 pm on New Year's Day, what is the latest time he can put the goose in the oven?

Nick has a poster on the wall in his office.

**ALWAYS GIVE 100%
AT WORK**

12% MONDAY
23% TUESDAY
40% WEDNESDAY
20% THURSDAY
5% FRIDAY

Nick's poster

**ALWAYS GIVE 100%
AT WORK**

14% MONDAY
18% TUESDAY
29% WEDNESDAY
36% THURSDAY
3% FRIDAY

Bernard's poster

Assuming that this poster refers to time, rather than effort, answer the following questions.

a If Nick actually worked this way, how long would he work on a Friday?

b How much longer would Nick work on a Wednesday compared with a Monday?

Bernard has a similar poster.

c Why can't you tell for certain who works for longer on a Tuesday?

Tip

You will need to decide how long a working day is. What is its usual length?

Joyce told her teacher that $y = x$ and $y = -x$ can be drawn as two straight lines that are perpendicular to each other.

The teacher asked Joyce what the gradient of each graph was.

a Complete Joyce's responses:

The gradient of $y = x$ is ... .

The gradient of $y = -x$ is ... .

The teacher asked Joyce to write down the equation of the line that has the same y-intercept as the graph $y = 2x - 3$, but which is perpendicular to it.

b Write the equation for the perpendicular line.

The teacher asked Joyce to write a statement on the board using the correct terminology to describe perpendicular lines, but to make it simple for the other students to remember.

c Write a statement for Joyce to write up for the class.

The probability of pop star Karri K releasing a song on a Thursday is 0.62.

If her song is released on a Thursday, the probability of this song becoming a number one single in the charts is 0.48.

If her song is released on any other day, the probability of it becoming a number one single is only 0.18.

What is the probability that Karri K will have a number one hit with the next song she releases?

Tip

What kind of diagram would be useful here?

A farmer has started making crisps to sell at the weekly farmers' market. She does not want to buy expensive packing equipment, so she asks her husband and son to pack the crisps for her each week. They must make each packet a similar weight.

At certain times the farmer does a random test on some of the packets.

These were the results one day:

Husband: 57.8 g, 61.1 g, 62.3 g, 58.9 g, 59.5 g, 60.6 g, 60.1 g, 58.8 g, 58.5 g, 61.3 g, 59.5 g

Son: 58.1 g, 58.7 g, 59.3 g, 58.9 g, 59.3 g, 58.8 g, 60.4 g, 59.1 g, 59.4 g, 58.9 g, 60.2 g

The packets need to be labelled with the weight. The farmer plans to label them as being 60 g. Is she right to do this? Give your reasons.

The table below shows data for the number of apples in a sample of 1 kg bags at two different supermarkets, A and B.

	A	B
Lower quartile	6	7
Median	9	8
Upper quartile	10	13

Which supermarket has the biggest apples? Justify your answer.

Pauline and Emma live in Salford and Woburn Sands respectively, two villages that are 12 km apart.

The girls plan to meet up on Saturday at Emma's house.

Pauline plans to walk to Woburn Sands, leaving home at 9.10. She can walk at a steady speed of 6 km/h.

Emma's mum will be cycling to Salford and should pass Pauline.

Emma's mum plans to leave Woburn Sands at 9.40. For the first 8 km, she will be travelling at 24 km/h, but the remainder of the route is very steep and she thinks she will not arrive in Salford until 10.40.

a When will Pauline meet Emma's mum?

b How far will Pauline be from home when they meet?

c How far will Emma's mum have travelled?

d What time is Pauline expecting to arrive at Emma's house?

e What is the speed Emma's mum was travelling up the steep hill? Give your answer to one decimal place.

f What distance apart are Pauline and Emma's mum at 10.20?

The graph below shows the journey of a car and a moped.

The moped rider travelled from Edinburgh to Glasgow.

The car driver took the same route to Glasgow but returned to Edinburgh.

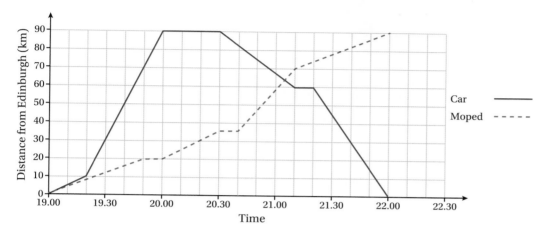

a How far did the moped rider travel in the first 25 minutes?

b How long did it take the car to travel the first 10 km? Can you explain the speed for this first stage of the journey?

c How many stops did the moped rider make and what was the total time she spent resting?

d What was the fastest stage of the journey for the car driver?

e What was the driver's speed at this fast stage?

f At roughly what time did the car and the moped pass each other?

g Roughly how far did the moped rider still have to go when she met the car driver?

h What was the average speed for the moped rider's whole journey?

i What was the average speed for the car driver's return journey?

Johnny says if the graph f(x) = 2x + 4 is transformed by $\begin{pmatrix} 0 \\ 7 \end{pmatrix}$, the intercept on the f(x) axis will become (0, 11).

Is Johnny correct?

Explain your answer.

Two spiders are in a room that is 4.5 m long, 3 m wide and 2 m high.

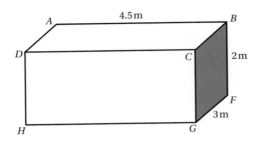

The male spider is at vertex A and the female spider is at vertex G.

a How far must the male spider crawl to get to the female if it only crawls along the edges of the room?

b If instead the male stays at A and the female spider travels along the diagonal of the face $GCDH$, then along edge DA to get to the male, how much shorter will her journey be?

Ryan draws a square of length 7.0 cm correct to the nearest millimetre. He then draws a circle that fits exactly inside the square.

Calculate the upper bound for the difference between the area of the circle and the area of the square.

 The following question is posed to a class:

Find an equivalent expression to $10 \times \sqrt{15}$.

The teacher takes the answers suggested by the first four students:

A: $\sqrt{150}$ B: $\sqrt{1500}$ C: 40   D: 35

Which, if any, of their values are correct? Explain your answer.

This sequence is generated by adding consecutive even numbers:

0, 2, 6, 12, 20, 30...

a Write down the next three terms.

b Find the nth term for the sequence.

c How does the algebra tell you that every term in the sequence must be even?

Cam keeps rabbits in his garden. They drink from two cylindrical water bottles, one small and one large.

The smaller bottle has a diameter of 8.5 cm and a height of 23 cm.

The larger bottle has a radius of 5.5 cm and a height of 25 cm.

How much **more** water does the larger bottle hold? Give your answer to the nearest millilitre.

Tip

Can you work out the volume of a cylinder? What is the link between cubic centimetres (cm^3) and millilitres?

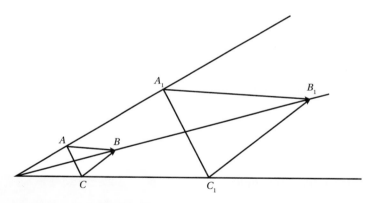

ABC and $A_1B_1C_1$ are similar triangles.

In the diagram above $\overrightarrow{AB} = 2a - b$, $\overrightarrow{CB} = a + 2b$ and $\overrightarrow{C_1B_1} = 3a + 6b$

a Express $\overrightarrow{AC}$ in terms of a and b.

b Express $\overrightarrow{A_1B_1}$ in terms of a and b.

A square-based pyramid is made so all of its edges are 2 m long.

Tip

How can you make right-angled triangles? How could this help?

a How high is the pyramid?

b Suppose the edges were all 3 m long. How high would it be now?

c What is the general rule for a pyramid of side length n metres?

All standard television screens are mathematically similar. The size of a TV screen is advertised as the diagonal length, in inches.

Carlos owns a 36.7-inch wide-screen TV and measures its width as 32.2 inches.

a What is the aspect ratio (ratio of width to height) for a wide-screen TV?

Eddie is buying a 42-inch wide-screen TV (where 42 inches is the length of the diagonal).

b Work out the length and width of his new TV. Give your answers to one decimal place.

A pair of tongs has arms 25 cm long. When not in use, the angle between the two arms is 60°.

Alison uses the tongs to pick up a meatball 5 cm in diameter.

By how much will the angle between the two arms be reduced?

Tip

Draw a diagram to help you see what is happening. Which topic will you need to use?

Robert is teaching his maths class about linear programming. He has a problem for them to solve, using small interconnecting bricks.

He gives each student eight red bricks and six yellow bricks and tells them to model a problem based on how many chairs and tables a company could make with a limited supply of materials.

Each table require two red bricks and two yellow bricks. Each chair requires two red bricks and one yellow brick.

Chair

Table

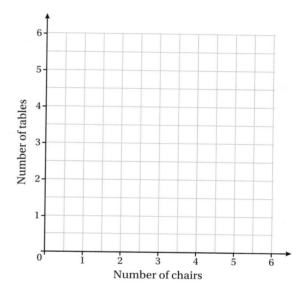

a Write an inequality to show the number of tables and chairs that could be made with the red bricks.

b Write an inequality to show the number of chairs and tables that could be made with the yellow bricks.

c Show these inequalities on the axes given.

a Would you expect there to be correlation between the average number of hours a secondary school student sleeps each night and the year group they are in?

b Write a hypothesis about this.

c Design a questionnaire to test your hypothesis.

d What type of diagram might be a useful way to display the data?

By how much could the volume of this cuboid vary if its side lengths were measured correct to:

a the nearest metre

b three significant figures

c the nearest millimetre?

The dial on Rupa's washing machine has a radius of 3.2 cm. It can be turned so that the arrow points to each of five equally spaced settings.

Rupa turns the dial clockwise from 0 through a curved arc of length 121 mm. Which setting has she chosen?

Tip

Think carefully about the sort of maths methods you need to use.

 Consider each pair of expressions and decide which is the larger.

a $\dfrac{3}{\sqrt{5}}$ or $\dfrac{5}{2\sqrt{5}}$

b $\dfrac{4}{\sqrt{8}}$ or $\dfrac{25}{\sqrt{50}}$

c $\dfrac{10}{\sqrt{7}+3}$ or $\dfrac{6}{\sqrt{7}-3}$

Tip

How do you compare fractions? Can you apply the same technique here?

Everything in Shop A is being sold at the same percentage discount.

Shop B is also selling all its stock at a discount, but it is not cutting its prices by as much.

A jacket now costs £209 in Shop A but £259 in Shop B. The recommended retail price (RRP) for the jacket is £310.

a What percentage discount from the RRP is being offered in each shop?

b A pair of trainers is priced at £62 in Shop A. How much will they cost in Shop B?

It is easy to get involved in working on a problem and forget that you can sometimes use common sense to tell roughly how big an answer ought to be. You will probably still need to do the calculations, but this can give you a useful guide as to whether an answer is correct or not.

In A Level Biology several formulae are used to calculate the actual size of something that has been viewed through a microscope.

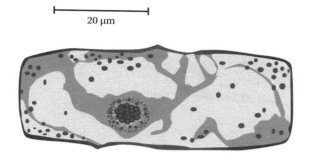

20 μm

The diagram above shows a cell. The students have worked out the actual width of the cell using the formulae, but some of them have got the wrong answer. However, you can tell which of these answers is correct, even if you aren't studying Biology.

a 5.6 μm   b 56 μm   c 560 μm   d 5600 μm

The line above the diagram is 20 μm long and the cell is about three times as wide as that line, so it must be about 60 μm. The answer must therefore be **b** = 56 μm.

A politician recently complained about the lack of depth of a particular policy. They described it as being 'a mile wide and an inch high'.

What is the area of a rectangle that is 'a mile wide and an inch high'? Give your answer in square metres.

You could begin by thinking about what a sensible sized answer would be. Would the area be equivalent to that of a tabletop, a classroom, school hall, playing field, or would it be even larger?

Jemal says:

Malcolm says:

'If I started with a ribbon that was an inch wide and a mile long, and cut it into strips, I think it would cover the classroom floor.'

'If I had a vacuum cleaner with a very thin nozzle (an inch wide!), how much carpet would I clean by the time I'd walked a mile? It takes about 20 minutes to walk one mile. If I was vacuuming for 20 minutes, I reckon I could cover about two rooms.'

You could make use of other problem-solving techniques, such as drawing a diagram like the one below (note that it is not to scale).

1 inch

1 mile

You will also need some knowledge about converting units. The conversions you need here are 1 mile = 1600 m and 1 inch = 2.5 cm.

To work out the area of the rectangle you need to multiply 1600 m by 2.5 cm, but you must use the same units for both measurements, so you can do 1600×0.025.

This will give the answer in m^2.

$1600 \, m \times 0.025 \, m = 40 \, m^2$

A room that is 5 m by 8 m would have a floor area of $40 \, m^2$ so it is about the size of a classroom, which does seem sensible.

The following problems may be solved using more than one method; however, the worked solutions provided at the back of this book are based on the method introduced above.

Running tracks come in two standard lengths. Indoor tracks are 200 m long and outdoor tracks are 400 m long.

a Simon's event is the 1500 m.

How many laps of each track will Simon run in his race?

b Denise will be running both the 5 km and 10 km race.

How many laps of each track will she run in each race?

The rule for calculating how long to cook a piece of lamb so that it is medium rare is '40 minutes per kilogram and an additional 25 minutes, at 180° C'.

a Create a formula to calculate the cooking time for a piece of lamb of any size cooked this way.

Uncle Bertie wants to serve Sunday lunch at 12.30 pm. His piece of lamb weighs 3.75 kg and it must stand for 10 minutes after it comes out of the oven.

b Uncle Bertie thinks he needs to put the lamb in the oven at 9 am. Is he right?

The ingredients for Fiona's chocolate cake recipe for eight people are shown below.

Cake	Icing
150 g dark chocolate	120 g dark chocolate
6 eggs	100 g hazelnuts
125 g unsalted butter	125 ml double cream
400 g chocolate spread	
100 g ground hazelnuts	

Fiona is having a dinner party with 20 guests. She wants to have enough cake for each guest to have one slice.

a How much dark chocolate should Fiona buy?

b The dark chocolate is available in 200 g bars. How many bars will she need?

c Express the amount of chocolate used to chocolate left over as a ratio in its simplest form.

d On another occasion, Fiona reduces the recipe to serve six people. How much chocolate spread does Fiona need?

Hattie does some form of exercise each day.

Each day she decides at random to do one of the following:
swim 40 lengths, jog 10 km or complete a two-hour cycle ride.

a Draw a sample space diagram showing all the possibilities of the exercise Hattie could do on two consecutive days.

b What is the probability that she swims on both days?

c What is the probability that she does not do the same exercise on both days?

Five cleaners can clean an office building in two hours and 45 minutes.

a How long should it take three cleaners to clean the building? Give your answer correct to the nearest minute.

b Each cleaner is paid the same hourly rate, and their time is rounded up to the next whole hour. Does reducing the number of cleaners from five to three reduce the amount paid in wages?

Two basketball coaches want to do a study of each of their teams and need the average height of all team members including reserves.

Coach McKay uses the data in the table on the right to find the mean height for his team.

Coach Cooksey uses the data from the last health check on each member of his team to find the mean height. The data are as follows:

150 cm, 156 cm, 187 cm, 199 cm, 203 cm, 178 cm, 194 cm, 188 cm, 167 cm, 194 cm, 152 cm, 226 cm, 225 cm, 199 cm, 188 cm, 221 cm, 178 cm, 143 cm, 142 cm, 170 cm.

a Which coach will have the more accurate mean height for his team? Explain your answer.

b What is the mean height for the McKay team?

c Compare the mean heights of the two teams. Make sure you use the data to justify your comparison.

Team McKay	
Height (cm)	**Frequency**
$145 \leqslant h < 155$	1
$155 \leqslant h < 165$	2
$165 \leqslant h < 175$	2
$175 \leqslant h < 185$	8
$185 \leqslant h < 195$	3
$195 \leqslant h < 225$	4

Two glasses of the same size contain orange drinks.

The first glass is $\frac{1}{4}$ squash and $\frac{3}{4}$ water.

The second glass is $\frac{1}{6}$ squash and $\frac{5}{6}$ water.

The two glasses are poured into a large drinks bottle.

a What fraction of the resulting drink is squash?

Amit is serving drinks at a party. He has two large jugs of fruit punch. The jugs are identical in size, but one contains punch that is $\frac{2}{5}$ apple juice and the other contains punch that is $\frac{3}{10}$ apple juice.

Amit wonders how the drink will change if he pours some from both jugs into a glass.

b Is it possible for Amit to create a drink that is exactly $\frac{1}{2}$ apple juice?

Valerie told Doug the expression for the area of the rectangle on the right is $x^2 - 7x + 6$.

Doug said she was wrong. He told Valerie the expression for the area was $2(2x - 7)$.

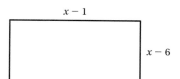

a Who is correct? Justify your answer.

Doug also (correctly) told Valerie the area was numerically 2 more than the perimeter. He explained as an example that if the perimeter was 12 cm, then the area would be 14 cm².

b What are the dimensions of the rectangle?

Valerie did her calculations and told Doug that x could have two values. She said x could equal 2 cm or 9 cm. Doug burst out laughing and told her to use logic to work out why this was not true.

c Explain why Doug found Valerie's statement funny.

A health campaign is targeting the high levels of sugar in low fat foods.

One particular brand of low fat yoghurt is sold in 104 g pots and contains 5.9 g of sugar.

Another yoghurt is sold in 90 g pots and contains 5% sugar.

If the guideline daily amount (GDA) of sugar for an adult is approximately 90 g, how do the two yoghurts compare?

Meg has 105 chocolate buttons. Grace has 95 chocolate buttons.

By what percentage will each girl need to change their number of chocolate buttons in order to have exactly 100 each?

Mr George has a box of board markers. It contains six blue markers, five black markers, seven green markers and two red markers. When he needs a marker, he picks one from the box at random, uses it and then places it back in the box.

On Monday Mr George needed a marker on two occasions.

What is the probability that he randomly:

a picked the same colour both times?

b picked a different colour the second time?

c If Mr George forgets to put the first marker back in the box, what is the probability now of taking the same colour of marker both times?

d Is the probability when he forgets to put it back higher or lower than when he remembers to put it back?

Peter is 2.03 m tall. He and his three shorter friends are planning on going camping. They will be using a traditional tent in the shape of a triangular prism.

What dimensions must their tent be so that Peter can stand upright comfortably and lie flat to sleep alongside his three friends?

Tip

You will need to make some assumptions in order to answer this question. You know how tall Peter is, but how much space will he need from side to side?

The cost of an extension to a house is directly proportional to the floor area of the extension. The floor area of an extension is 4 m by 5 m and its cost is £15 000.

a What is the largest floor area possible for £23 000 if the dimensions must be in complete metres?

The extension can be completed in four weeks if the builder has three labourers working five-day weeks from 8 am until 5 pm with him.

b How many labourers are needed to finish within three weeks?

c With the builder and this number of labourers, exactly when after their start day should the job be completed?

The labourers are paid a daily rate, and the builder has decided that the jobs left on the last day are best done by him on his own.

d How many extra hours would the builder be working without the labourers? Will the entire job still be completed within three weeks?

The labourers are paid a flat rate of £100 per day. The total price charged by the builder covers labour, materials and profit in the ratio 26 : 39 : 25.

e What percentage of the price charged is profit?

The table below shows the number of students in each year group at a new school.

Year 7	243
Year 8	176
Year 9	162
Year 10	88
Year 11	51

Tip

What would be the problem with each method?

It has been decided there should be a student council of 20 students.

The head teacher wants to take a stratified sample of 20 students to be on this student council.

The deputy head wants to have four students from each year group on the student council.

a If the head teacher uses her method, how many of each year group will be on the council?

b Give your opinion on the method you think is best.

Susanne wants some carpet fitted in her flat.

Two firms in her area specialise in floorings: Carpet Lay and Underfoot.

She has checked their websites and plotted their charges on a graph to compare their prices.

a How much does each company charge to lay 5 m² of carpet?

b Which company is the cheaper to fit 7.5 m² of carpet?

c What is the largest whole number of square metres that Carpet Lay would lay at a lower price than Underfoot?

Susanne needs a total of 9 m² of carpet laid.

d Which company should Susanne use?

e How much will this cost her?

The depth of water in Oban Bay depends on the time of day and the state of the tide.

Time (hours am)	0	1	2	3	4	5	6	7	8	9	10	11	12
Depth (metres)	7.0	10.7	12.0	12.1	10.5	7.5	4.6	2.6	1.5	1.2	1.9	4.1	8.0

a Copy the axes, plot the points and join them with a smooth curve.

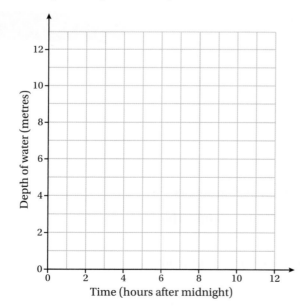

The Mull ferry needs at least 4 m of water to stay afloat.

b Between what times should it not attempt to dock?

c Is there going to be another period of 'danger' time within a 24-hour period?

The data in the table below show the number of microbes present in a petri dish after certain periods of time.

Number of microbes	315	1215	90	447	123	690	63	378	258
Number of minutes	10	20	5	12	6	15	4	11	9

a Estimate how many microbes were present after eight minutes.

b Is it possible to predict how many microbes might be present after 50 minutes? Explain your answer.

Mrs Grant decided to do a survey with her Year 7 class to find out how much time they spend playing games on their phones.

She recorded the average amount of time the students spent playing games each day.

a Copy and complete the histogram.

b Complete the frequency table.

Time (minutes)	Frequency
$10 < t \leqslant 20$	5
$20 < t \leqslant 60$	4
$60 < t \leqslant 120$	
$120 < t \leqslant 150$	3

Mrs Grant told the class that in her opinion anyone who spent more than 100 minutes per day playing the games probably wasn't spending enough time on their homework.

c How many students were not doing enough homework?

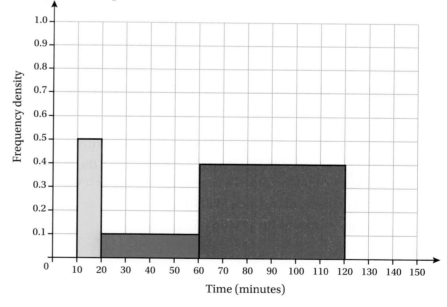

Sometimes it's useful to make a change to a diagram or situation so that it is easier to see what's going on.

> The diagram below shows a red square with a purple circle drawn through its vertices and a blue square drawn so it touches the purple circle on all sides.
>
> What is the relationship between the area of the red square and the area of the blue square? Explain how you know.

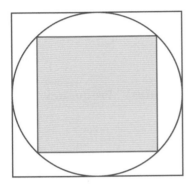

Before you turn the page, have a go at the question.

What ideas have you got?

Here are some things you can try:

- Get a rough idea of what the answer will be; you know that the blue square is bigger than the red square, but it is certainly less than, say, four times the area. This is **not** the way to work out the final answer, not least because you can't provide an explanation, but it will help you decide if your answer seems reasonable later.
- You don't know any measurements, so do you need to provide some?
- Will it help to call the side length of the red square x? The radius of the circle could be r. Maybe this will be useful and maybe it won't.
- Try putting on some extra lines. Will they help?

Did you manage to answer the problem?

Tip

If you can't do it don't worry. This is a mathematical problem that is supposed to be difficult. Remember, if you could 'see' the answer then it wouldn't be a mathematical 'problem'.

If not, here's one way that you could have solved it by changing the way you look at the diagram.

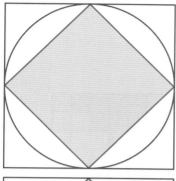

If you rotate the red square nothing vital changes.

The area of the red square is still the same and the purple and blue shapes are unaffected.

Does this help you to see the relationship between the red square and the blue square?

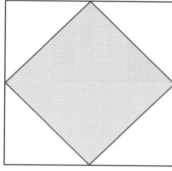

To make this very clear you can remove the circle.

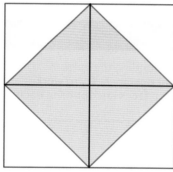

Then you can divide the shape up like this.

Tip

The extra lines are helpful after you've rotated the red square.

Now you can explain that the area of the red square is half the area of the blue square.

Here is an example of a full answer.

If you rotate the red square so the vertices of the red square meet the middle of the sides of the blue square you do not change its area.

The two extra lines I have added join the vertices of the red square, cutting it into quarters that are right-angled triangles. These lines also join the middle of the sides of the blue square, cutting it into quarters that are squares.

The total area of the red right-angled triangles is half the area of the blue square.

So the area of the red square is half the area of the blue square.

Tip

You had a rough idea that the area of the blue square was between one and four times the area of the red square, and it is. Estimating the answer can be a useful check that your final answer is sensible.

Tip

You may have answered this question by working out some measurements in terms of x or r instead. This is also a good way to solve the problem.

Here is another question.

> The formula for a triangular number is $T = \frac{1}{2}n(n+1)$.
>
> Prove that $8T + 1$ is always a square number.

This can be done algebraically:

$$8T + 1 = 8 \times \frac{1}{2}n(n+1) + 1$$
$$= 4n^2 + 4n + 1$$

This factorises to give $(2n+1)^2$, which is square.

An alternative method is to use a diagram.

There are clearly 8 copies of a triangular number, there is 1 in the middle and it makes a square. To complete this explanation you need to show that it will work for all triangular numbers.

The following problems may be solved using more than one method; however, the worked solutions provided at the back of this book are based on the method introduced above.

Here are six views of the same cube.

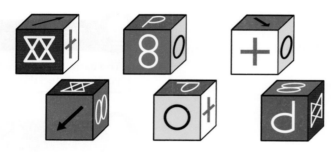

Which symbol is opposite the red cross?

> **Tip**
>
> Imagine holding the cube in different positions. Try to work out which faces are opposite each other.

Yasmin is looking at a 3-D solid. If she looks at it directly from the side this is what she sees:

If Yasmin now looks at it from directly above, what could she see?

How many different answers are there?

Describe the shapes as accurately as possible.

3 ★ ✿ ✿

A positive number is four more than five times its reciprocal.

a What is the number?

Another positive number is five more than six times its reciprocal.

b What is this number?

c What is $n - 1$ more than n times its reciprocal? Explain how you know.

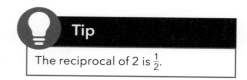

Tip

The reciprocal of 2 is $\frac{1}{2}$.

4 ★ ✿ ✿

Sections of decorative fencing are made with metal and wooden rods.

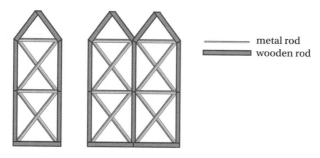

— metal rod
▬ wooden rod

a How many metal rods will be needed in the next pattern?

b How many wooden rods are needed for the fourth pattern?

c Find the number of metal rods needed for the nth pattern.

The metal rods cost £2 each and the wooden rods cost £2.50 each.

d Sue needs a fence consisting of 12 sections. How much will this cost?

5 ★ ✿ ✿

 Would you rather:

a receive 80% of £10 or 75% of £12?

b have 50% of one chocolate cake or 25% of two chocolate cakes?

c buy a CD in store for £12.99 or buy it online with a 5% discount code but a postage charge of £1.99?

6 ★ ✿ ✿

Susan is y years old. Mark is x years old.

Together their ages total 20 years.

Susan is 8 years older than Mark.

How old are Susan and Mark?

Arthur has just bought a circular dining table of diameter 240 cm. It comes flat-packed to make it easier to transport. His front door is a rectangle, 2.1 m tall and 1.05 m wide. Will he be able to fit the tabletop through the door?

Tip

It should be clear that the circular table is not going to fit through the door if held vertically or horizontally. Arthur will need to tilt it to try to get it inside.

The number of living bacteria cells on a petri dish in the science lab is inversely proportional to the number of hours the dish remains in the refrigerator.

The number of living bacteria cells on a petri dish that has been in the refrigerator for four hours is 20 000.

Tommy told Jamila there would be 40 000 bacteria cells still growing on a petri dish that had been in the refrigerator for eight hours.

Jamila disagreed, saying that the longer the time in the refrigerator, the fewer the number of bacteria cells. Jamila worked out the number of bacteria cells she thought would be on the dish.

a Find a formula Jamila could use.

b What number of bacteria cells does Jamila's formula give for a dish that has been in the refrigerator for eight hours?

c What problems are there with Jamila's formula?

Simon is a landscape gardener and he needs to hire a small digger for his next job.

The cost of hiring a digger from JCEs is shown as a straight-line graph.

MoveIt Builders also hire out diggers, but they have a basic fixed charge in addition to their daily charge. Their charges are also shown as a straight-line graph.

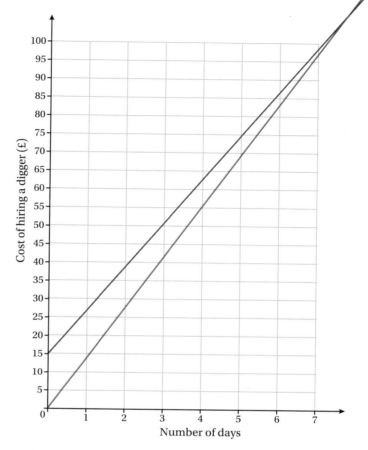

a Which line refers to the charges for each of the companies?

b What is the basic fixed charge made by one of the companies?

c How much per day do JCEs charge?

d Is MoveIt Builders' daily charge more or less than what JCEs charge? By how much?

e What would be the total cost if Simon hired the digger from MoveIt Builders for five days?

f What would be the total cost if Simon needed the digger for two weeks and he hired it from Move It Builders?

g If Simon needed the digger for two weeks, would it be cheaper from MoveIt Builders or JCEs?

h For the two-week period, how much less would it cost to hire from the cheaper company?

Jenny is given a set of instructions to create an image:

Mark a point on your page and label it 'O'.

Draw a 1 cm square with its bottom left-hand corner 1 cm to the right of O.

Enlarge this square by a scale factor of 2 about O.

Translate the smaller square 1 cm to the left.

Rotate the two smaller squares 90° clockwise about the centre of the larger square.

Rotate the image (up to and including the fifth step) 180° about the centre of the larger square.

a What should Jenny's completed image look like?

b How many lines of symmetry does the resulting image have?

c What order of rotational symmetry does the resulting image have?

d Design a set of instructions to create the image on the right.

Sarah draws the graph of $f(x) = (x - 2)(x + 2)$.

Sarah decides that if she made the transformation $\binom{0}{4}$ on her graph she would be sketching the graph of $f(x) = x^2$.

Is Sarah correct? Explain your answer.

Eric is reorganising the hamsters in his pet shop.

If he puts three in each cage, there is one hamster left with no cage to go into.

If he puts four in each cage, one cage is left empty.

a How many hamsters does Eric have?

b How many cages does he have?

a Find three consecutive even numbers that add up to 228.

b Find three consecutive odd numbers that add up to 291.

c The sum of the squares of two consecutive numbers is 1301. Find the numbers.

d The difference between two numbers is 6. The sum of the two numbers is 80. Find the numbers.

 Compare each pair of numbers and decide which symbol out of <, >, or = should be placed in between them.

a $\frac{2}{3}$ 0.66   **b** 0.25 $\frac{8}{32}$

c $\frac{3}{11}$ 0.273   **d** 0.05 $\frac{1}{22}$

e 0.5   0.4999...

What conditions are there on the values of x and y if a can be anything and each equation is always correct?

a $(a^x)^y = 1$

b $(a^x)^y = a$

c $(a^x)^y = \sqrt{a}\ (a \geqslant 0)$

Anna is planning to do something silly to raise money for charity.

Will it be cheaper for her to take a bath in cola or in baked beans?

Tip

Remember that: $1\,ml = 1\,cm^3$.

0.15 m³

Beans
400 ml

54p

1l £1.49

The area of a square is given as $4x^2 - 12x + 9$.

Find an expression for the perimeter of the square.

a Create a formula, in terms of x, to calculate the area of the shaded border.

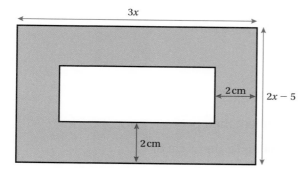

3x

2 cm

2x − 5

2 cm

b The area of the border is 204 cm². What are the dimensions of the outer rectangle?

The sequence 2, 10, 24, 44, 70... can be written as (1×2), (2×5), (3×8), (4×11), (5×14)...

a Write an expression for the nth term of the sequence.

b One of the terms in the sequence is 234.

Write this term in the form $(a \times b)$, where a and b are values to be determined.

Aaron went to the local fruit market and bought four apples and five bananas for £2.05.

Peter went to the same fruit market and bought three apples and seven bananas for £2.35.

Aaron and Peter asked their maths teacher for an easy method to find the price of an apple and the price of a banana.

She told them they could create an equation for the cost of the fruit each of them bought and solve them simultaneously.

a Write the two equations.

b What is the cost of an apple?

c What is the price of a banana?

d Can you show this same information as straight-line graphs? How would you use your graphs to find the price of the apple and the banana?

100 people were asked to complete a questionnaire about their pets.

Out of the 100 people, 17 had both a cat and a dog. 54 had either a cat or a dog, but not both. 30 people owned a dog.

a If one person was chosen at random, what is the probability they had neither a cat nor a dog?

b If one person was chosen at random, what is the probability they only owned a cat?

22

The planet Mars takes 24.6 hours to rotate on its axis. The Earth takes 24 hours to rotate on its axis.

a Express these times in hours as ratios in their simplest form (Mars : Earth, in integer form).

b Express these times in minutes as ratios in their simplest form.

The mass of Mars is 6.4×10^{23} kg. The mass of Earth is 6.0×10^{24} kg.

c Express the masses as ratios.

The highest mountain in the Solar System is Olympus Mons, measuring approximately 27 km. Olympus Mons is on Mars. The highest mountain on Earth, Mount Everest, is 8848 m.

d Using a suitable degree of accuracy, express the heights as ratios (Olympus Mons : Mount Everest).

23

Triangles *ABC* and *XYZ* are similar shapes.

 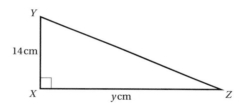

In triangle *ABC*, length *AB* is 8 cm and *AC* is 20 cm.

In triangle *XYZ*, length *XY* is 14 cm and *XZ* is *y* cm.

a Work out the area of triangle *XYZ*.

b Express area of triangle *ABC* : area of triangle *XYZ* in its simplest form.

c What type of numbers are in the ratio? Can you explain this?

24

In how many ways can you get from flag **A** to flag **B**:

a using a single transformation?

b using exactly two transformations?

 Tip

Remember to provide all the information necessary to describe each transformation fully.

a Complete the table of values for the graph $f(x) = x^2 - 6x - 5$.

x	–2	–1	0	1	2	3	4	5	6
$f(x)$									

b Write down the coordinates of the turning point of the function $f(x)$.

c Write down the exact values of the roots of the function $f(x)$.

d Write down the coordinates of the turning point of the function $-f(x)$.

e Write down the exact values of the roots of the function $-f(x)$.

Zain wanted to do the transformation $f(x - 8)$ on the function $f(x) = x^3$. He wrongly used the translation vector $\begin{pmatrix} 0 \\ -8 \end{pmatrix}$.

a Explain why this is wrong.

b Starting from Zain's new, incorrect version, what translation vector should he use to get to the correct answer?

Brandon is learning about the sine and cosine graphs.

His teacher asked Brandon to sketch both the sine and cosine graphs, showing all coordinates of the points where the graphs cross the axes.

a Sketch the sine graph and the cosine graph on the same set of axes.

His teacher then asked Brandon to describe the sine graph in terms of a transformation of the graph of $f(x) = \cos(x)$.

b Write down this transformation.

The teacher then asked Brandon to change it around and to describe the cosine graph in terms of a transformation on the sine graph.

c Write down this transformation.

d Would you describe these transformations as reflections or translations?

A square is surrounded by four identical rectangular tiles, as shown.

a Find an expression for the total area of the four identical tiles.

b Find an expression for the area of the large square.

c What is the area of the unshaded square?

In an exam, students are asked to calculate the area of the shape shown below (a semicircle and an isosceles triangle). They are instructed to give their answer correct to one decimal place.

Tip

Ollie's answer is very close. Why is it not exact?

Ollie's answer is shown here:

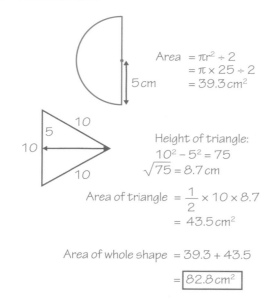

Area $= \pi r^2 \div 2$
$= \pi \times 25 \div 2$
$= 39.3\,cm^2$

Height of triangle:
$10^2 - 5^2 = 75$
$\sqrt{75} = 8.7\,cm$

Area of triangle $= \dfrac{1}{2} \times 10 \times 8.7$
$= 43.5\,cm^2$

Area of whole shape $= 39.3 + 43.5$
$= \boxed{82.8\,cm^2}$

The examiner marks Ollie's answer as incorrect, although he awards some marks for Ollie's method.

a What is the problem with Ollie's answer?

b What is the answer that the examiner was looking for?

A square piece of paper, of side length 8 cm, is folded so that the bottom right-hand corner, *C*, meets the midpoint of the top edge *AB*.

Tip

Remember that for similar triangles you only need to consider the angles.

 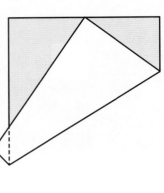

a Show that the three triangles created are mathematically similar.

b Show that the lengths of the sides of the smallest triangle are exactly a quarter the size of the largest triangle.

 a Use the diagram of an equilateral triangle to find the exact value of:

i tan 60°   **ii** sin 60°   **iii** cos 60°.

Tip

What do you know about the properties of an equilateral triangle?
Why is the triangle divided in half?

b How does this diagram show that sin 60° = cos 30°.

In some problems you need to make sure you get every possible answer, without missing or repeating any.

Here is the flag of South Korea.

Around the edge of the central circle there are four 'trigrams'. These are made up of three lines. The one on the right has three solid lines.

And this one has a broken line at the bottom and the top, with a solid line in the middle.

If you just use solid and broken lines, what fraction of all the possible trigrams (made using three lines) appear on the South Korean flag?

First of all, do you understand the problem? There are other trigrams that haven't yet been drawn, such as the one on the right.

It looks as if you will need to work out how many possibilities there are. If you just start writing them down (which is a reasonable starting point) there is a risk that you will miss or repeat some of them.

These are the ones you have got so far:

A better way to do this would be to work systematically. You could start with three solid lines and no broken lines. That is easy because there is only one of them as shown on the right.

Next you could have two solid lines and one broken line:

This example is systematic in the way the broken line has moved downwards. Can you finish off the rest of the trigrams?

The final list that you get is as follows:

There are eight of them and you can be confident that because you have worked systematically you haven't missed any out, or got any of them twice.

Go back to the original question: **What fraction of all the possible trigrams (made using three lines) appear on the South Korean flag?**

There are four of them on the flag and you know there are eight altogether, so $\frac{1}{2}$ of the trigrams appear on the flag. (Rather neatly, they have chosen to use the four that look the same, both ways up!) If you want to test your ability to work systematically try to find all the ways to make trigrams that use four lines.

Sometimes we can work systematically but save ourselves some time. Here's an example.

> The postman knew it was Mrs Stanley's birthday because of the large number of cards and packages he had to deliver. When he asked Mrs Stanley how old she was, she told him: 'Yesterday my age was a square number, but today it is a prime number.' Can the postman work out how old Mrs Stanley is?

You need to find two consecutive numbers where the first one is a square number (yesterday's age) and the next number is a prime number (Mrs Stanley's age today, on her birthday).

Guessing numbers at random doesn't seem sensible. You could either list the prime numbers and find out whether the number before them all is a square number, or you could do it the other way round and list all the square numbers and see whether the next number is prime.

Both methods will work, but you should use the second one because working out some square numbers is much easier than listing prime numbers.

So far this is looking good. You are working systematically through the numbers and haven't missed any out.

You might have realised that you don't need to check the odd square numbers from now on (so the rows 7 and 9 in the table on the right have been shaded out), because when you add 1 the number will be even and can't be prime.

Which numbers work? Mrs Stanley could be 2, 5, 17, 37 or 101 years old. She is an adult, so that means she is either 37 or 101. Hopefully it would be obvious from Mrs Stanley's appearance whether she is 37 or 101, so it is likely that the postman **can** work out how old she is.

The following problems may be solved using more than one method; however, the worked solutions provided at the back of this book are based on the method introduced above.

n	Square number (n^2)	Add one to this	Is it prime?
1	1	2	Yes
2	4	5	Yes
3	9	10	No
4	16	17	Yes
5	25	26	No
6	36		
7	49		
8	64		
9	81		
10	100		

n	Square number (n^2)	Add one to this	Is it prime?
1	1	2	Yes
2	4	5	Yes
3	9	10	No
4	16	17	Yes
5	25	26	No
6	36	37	Yes
7	49		
8	64	65	No
9	81		
10	100	101	Yes

The first two questions on a worksheet are:

a Using positive integers less than 10, how many different addition questions could be on the rest of the worksheet? (Note the order in addition is not important, so 4 + 2 is the same as 2 + 4, and therefore these do not count as different questions.)

b If the worksheet includes negative integers greater than –10, how many different answers to addition calculations could there be?

 Insert the operators +, – and × into the three boxes below. You should use each of them once.

5 ☐ 2 ☐ 10 ☐ –3

In how many ways can you achieve a negative result?

Martin helps himself to sandwiches from a buffet lunch. He notices that the sandwiches have all been cut into identical triangles.

> **Tip**
>
> Think of a logical way of trying out all the possible arrangements of the sandwiches.
>
> You also need to decide on a sensible way to record your findings so that you can be sure you have found all the possible polygons.

Martin places his sandwiches so that they fit together to create a square. He wonders how many different polygons he can create by arranging two or more sandwiches on his plate.

a Assuming that Martin matches the edges of the sandwiches, how many different polygons can he create, using:

   i exactly two sandwiches

   ii exactly three sandwiches

   iii all four sandwiches?

b Is it possible for Martin to create all the special types of quadrilateral, using two or more sandwiches from his plate?

$a + b = 1$

How many different pairs of values of a and b will satisfy this equation if:

a a and b are non-negative integers

b a and b are positive decimal numbers with one decimal place

c a and b are positive decimal numbers with two decimal places

d   How would your answer to part **a** change if a and b were allowed to take negative values?

Tip

Write out the answers in a systematic way.

The fractions $\frac{2}{3}$ and $\frac{1}{5}$ can be combined using any of +, −, × and ÷.

a   What is the biggest answer you can get?

b   What is the smallest possible answer?

A factory makes packing boxes for cylinders.

Each box is a cuboid measuring 40 cm × 40 cm with a height of 15 cm.

a   What are the maximum dimensions (radius and height) of the cylinders that can fit into each box?

b   Make a guess as to which box has the most unused space.

c   Use calculations to check your guess. What did you find?

Tip

The volume of a cylinder is $\pi \times r^2 \times h$.

Tip

The strategy from Chapter 8 could be helpful here. You can ignore the height of the cylinders because it is the same for all of them.

Shona has five cards from a pack of playing cards: two jacks, a queen, a king and an ace. She shuffles the cards and picks two at random.

a   Make a list of all possible pairs of cards she could pick.

b   What is the probability she picks the two jacks?

c   What is the probability she does not pick any jacks?

For a set of ten numbers the following information is known:

Mode = 3, range = 10, median = 3, mean = 6.

The numbers are all integers and there are only three different integers involved.

a Can you find the ten numbers?

For another set of four odd numbers the mean is 20, the mode is 3 and the median is 3.

b What are the numbers?

In this second set of four numbers, some changes are made. The numbers are still all odd, the mode is still 3, but the median is now 5.

c What numbers are now in this set?

The numbers are changed again, so the four odd numbers have a mode of 3 and a median of 10.

d What are the numbers in this set now?

e What happens if the mode of four odd numbers is 3 and the median is 15?

f Investigate all possible sets of four odd numbers with a mode of 3 and mean of 20.

Tip

Working systematically can help you spot a pattern here. Remember: The median must always remain an integer.

Jeff draws a heptagon and numbers the vertices in order. He then draws a diagonal on the shape and adds up the numbers at the ends of the diagonal. He then repeats the process with another diagonal.

So far Jeff has a total of 21 (5 + 10 + 6).

Jeff draws all the possible diagonals and adds the numbers on.

a What is his final total?

Phil does the same thing with a hexagon.

Ali does the same thing with a pentagon.

b If Phil and Ali add their totals together, will they have a bigger number than Jeff?

Tip

A diagonal of a shape joins two vertices that are not next to each other.

Two numbers are called co-prime if their highest common factor (HCF) is 1. For example, 9 and 10 are co-prime, but 10 and 14 are not (they have an HCF of 2).

You choose two numbers from 1 to 12. The order is not important and you can have the same number twice.

a There are 78 such pairs. Show how you know this is correct.

b What fraction of the integer pairs from 1 to 12 are co-prime?

Find values for a, b and c that make this equation true:

$245 = 1^a + 2^b + 3^c$

A splash pool is to be made from two interlocking circular holes, each of diameter 4 m.

The centres of the circles are 2 m apart.

The cost of the pool is broken down into the base (which is £800 per square metre) and the sides (£225 per metre of edge).

Work out the cost of the pool.

Calculate the missing length in the diagram below.

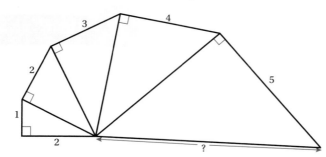

> **Tip**
>
> Work with one triangle at a time. Why is the working easier if you leave your calculations in surd form?

To make an ordinary cake you mix the ingredients together and then bake the mixture.

A friendship cake mixture is different. You add a little extra milk each day and only bake some of the mixture.

Molly starts a new friendship cake mixture.

After a week, Molly divides her mixture into four, keeps one portion for herself and gives the other three portions to friends.

Her friends keep their mixture for a week, feeding and stirring it each day.

After a week, everyone divides their mixture into four portions, keeps one of them and gives the other three portions to other friends.

This process can continue for weeks.

After one week Molly has given some of the original mixture away, so four people have got some mixture.

a How many people have the mixture after four weeks?

b How many will have the mixture after six weeks?

c The population of the UK is about 66 million. How many weeks would it take for everyone to receive Molly's friendship cake mixture?

d Why is it not likely that everyone would receive it?

 The equivalent decimal of every proper fraction is either terminating (it stops) or is recurring (it repeats forever).

How many of the fractions $\frac{1}{N}$, where N can take the value of any positive integer from 1 to 10, are recurring when you find their decimal equivalents?

Solve this problem without a calculator.

Tip

Remember that a fraction represents a division calculation. You could use short division or another written method to turn each fraction into a decimal. Make sure you continue for long enough to decide whether the fraction represents a terminating or recurring decimal.

If you are having difficulties with a problem, you might encounter a strange situation. You could call it 'the problem with problem solving' as shown in the illustration on the right.

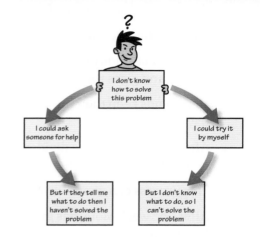

If you find yourself in this situation, one strategy you could try is: 'If you don't know what to do, do something.'

But make sure the 'something' you do is useful.

Some things that are **not** useful include colouring a picture (unless it is a problem about colouring) or writing the question out in perfect handwriting. These are just things that keep you busy, but are unlikely to help.

The previous chapters in this book outlined different problem-solving strategies. If you are stuck, try one of these strategies. If the first strategy you try doesn't work, try a different one.

You might find it helpful to write down the things you do know (for example the key ideas from the question) and which areas of mathematics these relate to.

Ben bought a bag of rice at the supermarket. He wonders how many grains of rice there are in the bag. Can you help him?

All sorts of things seem to make this question impossible to answer.

- Not every bag of rice has exactly the same number of grains of rice in it.
- Different varieties of rice are different sizes (for example, long grain rice is longer than risotto rice).
- Individual grains vary in size.
- We don't know how big the bag is. If he has bought a 1 kg bag then there will be approximately twice as many grains as in a 500 g bag.

You will have realised by now that there isn't going to be an exact answer, so you need to work out a rough answer. It is often useful to work out a ball-park figure, and as long as it is of the right order of magnitude (which means it has roughly the correct number of digits) then that will be reasonable.

If you decide a problem is difficult and do nothing then it won't get solved! You could start to try some things that might be useful.

Count every grain of rice in a bag.

Nice idea, but you haven't got a bag of rice and the answer is probably rather big, so it will take a long time. Besides, that involves counting rather than doing maths, so let's try something else.

Weigh a single grain and then work out how many grains there will be in 1 kg.

This is nicer, no counting involved! A 2p coin weighs 7 g, so a single grain of rice will be extremely light, and certainly less than 1 g. Your scales aren't accurate enough to do this (and you don't have any rice to weigh anyway).

Find out how many grains weigh 1 g and then multiply by 1000.

This is useful because it uses the fact that 1000 g = 1 kg. But you still don't have any rice to weigh.

Find out how big a grain of rice is.

Can you draw a picture of an uncooked grain of rice? (Uncooked rice is smaller than the fluffy, cooked rice.) The grains in the drawing on the right are about half a cm long and maybe 2 mm high.

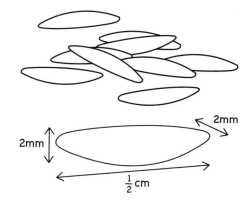

What shape is a grain of rice?

It's a bit like a cylinder but with sloping ends. In fact, it is roughly a cuboid! You could work out the rough volume of the grain of rice by assuming it is a cuboid that is $\frac{1}{2}$ cm by 2 mm by 2 mm.

Work out the volume of a bag of rice and compare this with the volume of a grain of rice. In the kitchen cupboard at home you are probably used to seeing 1 kg bags of food (sugar, flour, pasta, rice, etc). You can visualise a 1 kg bag of sugar. Using your ruler to help, visualise the size, which is about 10 cm by 15 cm by 8 cm.

But the units are all different. That is awkward, so you should work in mm.

The volume of a single grain of rice is about 5 mm × 2 mm × 2 mm. This is 20 mm³.

The volume of the bag is about 100 mm × 150 mm × 80 mm. This is 1 200 000 mm³.

1 200 000 ÷ 20 = 60 000, so there are roughly 60 000 grains in a bag.

Ask yourself whether this seems reasonable.

If 60 000 grains of rice weigh 1 kg then about 60 of them would weigh 1 g. So this does seem possible. The errors in your estimate of the sizes are likely to be outweighed by the fact that rice grains are not cuboids, but they also don't fit together perfectly in the bag.

To start with you had no idea what to do. You tried out some different ideas and eventually worked out an answer.

The following problems may be solved using more than one method; however, the worked solutions provided at the back of this book are based on the method introduced above.

Jyoti and Indira are making towers with cubes.

Between them they have 12 cubes, each of different sizes.

There is a 1 cm cube, a 2 cm cube, a 3 cm cube, a 4 cm cube and so on up to the biggest cube, which measures 12 cm along each edge.

For the first towers they make, Jyoti uses the six smallest cubes and Indira uses the six largest.

a How much taller is Indira's tower compared with Jyoti's?

The girls then decide to make towers of the same height using six cubes each.

b Work out a combination of cubes that each girl could have.

 Which of the statements about the number 12 345 678 912 are true?

i It is odd.

ii It is a multiple of 3.

iii It is a prime number.

iv Dividing the number by 5 leaves a remainder of 2.

v It is a multiple of 4.

Grandad Jones is twice as old as his son Geoff. Geoff was 29 years old when his own son Paul was born.

The combined age of the three family members is 131 years.

Find the ages of Grandad, Geoff and Paul.

The combined age of three family members is 134 years.

Raj is five times as old as his daughter Savita.

His wife Lata is nine years Raj's junior.

How old is Lata?

New safeguarding rules for schools state that there must be one accompanying teacher for every eight students going on a trip.

a 140 students plan to go on a trip to the London Dungeons. How many teachers will need to be on this trip?

b Other staff members have decided they want to join the trip. There are now 21 staff members available. How many extra students could go on the trip?

c It was too late to take extra students, so the original 140 students went with the extra staff. What is the new ratio of students to staff?

The school hired some 42-seater coaches to transport everyone.

The drivers also went into the Dungeons and so there are even more adults on the trip.

d Including the drivers, what is the new ratio of students to adults?

e What fraction of the group are now adults?

Two identical triangles are drawn using two diameters and two vertical lines, inside a circle of radius 7 cm.

If this diagram is placed on a coordinate grid so that the centre of the circle is located at the origin, what will be the coordinates of points A and B?

7

For a set of eight integers the following information is known:

The biggest number is 16.

Mean = 7.5. Mode = 3 and 5. Range = 15.

a Can you find the other numbers in the set?

b How many different solutions are there?

Tip

You know how many numbers there are. Draw boxes for them and then write in what you know.

8

In a set of five positive integers the range is 15, the mode is 2 and the median is 5.

a If the mean is 7, what are the numbers?

b If the range, mode and median stay the same, what is the biggest possible mean value if this is an integer value?

c If the range, mode and median stay the same, what is the smallest possible mean value?

9

$3 = \dfrac{a}{b} + c$

a, b and c are integers.

a Suggest values of a, b and c that will make the calculation correct.

b Suggest values of a, b and c that will make the calculation correct where b > 1.

c Suggest values of a, b and c that will make the calculation correct where b < 0.

10

 A magic square has numbers in each row, column and diagonal that add up to the same thing (the 'magic number').

For the magic square below the magic number is 2.1.

Tip

Copy the diagram and fill in the cells as you work them out.

0.74		
$\dfrac{129}{150}$		
		$\dfrac{33}{50}$

Complete the magic square.

Alesha has a pack of 52 playing cards. She picks one card at random, puts it on the table and then picks a second card.

Is it more likely that Alesha will get two aces or two red kings?

How much more likely?

 Tip

Would a diagram help? What about simplifying the problem so she picks just one card?

Adam has two pairs of grey socks, three pairs of brown socks, a blue pair and a stripey pair. He also has four ties. His ties are pink, blue, purple and grey.

Adam takes a pair of socks and a tie at random each morning.

What is the probability that:

a He takes a pair of grey socks and the pink tie?

b He takes the stripey socks and the purple tie?

c He takes grey socks and a matching tie?

d He takes socks and a tie of the same colour?

e He takes socks and a tie of different colours?

 Tip

What sort of diagram might be helpful here?

Rabbits can have four to eight kits (baby rabbits) in each litter.

The probability of how many kits any female rabbit might have in a litter is given in the table below.

Number of kits per litter	4	5	6	7	8
Probability	0.1	0.2	0.3	0.3	x

a What is the value of x in the table?

b What is the probability that two rabbits chosen at random will have a total of 16 kits?

c What is the probability that two randomly picked female rabbits have a total of ten kits in one breeding season?

14

There are approximately 5×10^9 red blood cells per millilitre of blood. James' blood volume is approximately 9 pints.

One pint is equal to 568 ml.

If James donates 10% of his blood, how many red blood cells has he still got?

15

a Explain how the pair of triangles shown below could be used to show that $\sqrt{8} = 2\sqrt{2}$.

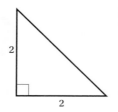

Diagrams not to scale

b Draw a pair of triangles to demonstrate that:

$\sqrt{18} = 3\sqrt{2}$

> **Tip**
>
> What can you work out?

> **Tip**
>
> Why is it useful that the two triangles are right-angled? The two triangles are mathematically similar. What does this mean and how can it help you?

16

Juliet is inviting some friends for afternoon tea. She wants to make chocolate brownies and lemonade.

In her mother's cupboard there is 350 g of sugar. Each glass of lemonade needs 30 g of sugar and each brownie requires 20 g of sugar.

Let x represent the number of glasses of lemonade and y represent the number of brownies.

a Write an inequality to show how much lemonade and how many brownies Juliet could make.

Juliet expects her friends will each have one glass of lemonade and one brownie.

b Write an inequality to show the number of friends Juliet could invite.

The manager of the local cinema did not want to give his employees a pay raise. He said on average they were earning more than the weekly national average wage, which is £130 per week.

Weekly wage in £	Frequency
61–80	2
81–100	5
101–150	9
151–200	2
201–250	1
251–300	1

a Why would finding the median wage not be helpful for the manager?

Feeling under pressure, the manager decided to increase the weekly wages of his two lowest paid employees to put them in the £81–100 wage bracket.

b How have these pay rises affected the average wage of the employees? What has happened?

A field is 80 m long by 70 m wide. A goat is tethered to a pole in the centre of the field by a rope 15 m long.

A farmer plants wheat across the width of the field for 30 m from one end. The goat eats all the wheat it can reach.

It costs £65 to plant a 1 m strip of wheat the width of the field, and the farmer makes a return of £4.50 per square metre harvested. The farmer plants strips along the complete width of the field, but he does not move the goat.

The farmer still makes a profit. How much profit?

Harvey carried out a combination of transformations on a starting shape on a centimetre-square grid:

Translate by the vector $\begin{pmatrix} 2 \\ -1 \end{pmatrix}$.

Rotate 90° clockwise about (1, 0).

All but Harvey's final image is hidden under a piece of paper.

What will the diagram look like when the paper is lifted?

Tip

How can you work backwards through this problem? What are the 'inverse' transformations that need to be applied?

20 ★ ★ ★

A piece of paper is folded to make a kite as shown in the diagram on the right.

The side lengths of the original piece of paper are in the ratio $1 : \sqrt{2}$.

Calculate the perimeter of the kite.

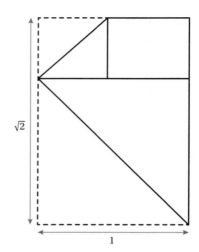

Diagram not to scale

$\sqrt{2}$

1

21 ★ ★ ★

The formula for the kinetic energy KE (in joules, J) of an object of mass m (in kg), travelling at a speed v (m/s), is:

$$KE = (\tfrac{1}{2})mv^2$$

Two students calculate the kinetic energy of a tennis ball of mass 56 g after it is served at a speed of 120 miles per hour.

Their answers are shown below:

Student 1:

$KE = (\tfrac{1}{2})mv^2 = (\tfrac{1}{2}) \times 56 \times 120^2 = 403\,200\,J$

Student 2:

The mass of the tennis ball needs to be changed into kg.

$56\,g = 0.056\,kg$

The speed of the tennis ball needs to be changed into metres per second. Using the conversion 5 miles = 8 km:

$\frac{120}{5} = 24$

$24 \times 8 = 192$ so $120\,mph = 192\,km/h$

$192\,km/h = 192\,000\,m/h$

There are $60 \times 60 = 3600$ seconds in one hour.

$\frac{192\,000}{3600} = 53.3333\ldots\,m/s$

$KE = 0.5\,mv^2$

$0.5 \times 0.056 \times 53.3 = 1.4924$

$1.4924^2 = 2.227\ldots$

So $= KE = 2.2\,J.$

Tip

Try answering the question yourself.

Both students have done some things correctly in their calculations but have ended up with the wrong answer.

Explain how each student should alter their method to achieve the correct result of 79.6 J.

1 a

An expression for the perimeter is $6x + 4$

To work out the perimeter of a rectangle, you need to add up the sides.

A diagram will help.

b An expression for the area is $(2x + 3)(x - 1)$

To work out the area you multiply the two sides.

c The perimeter is 70 cm, so $6x + 4 = 70$.

$x = 11$

Solve $6x + 4 = 70$ for x.

To work out the area you multiply the two sides.
The longest side is $2x + 3 = 2 \times 11 + 3$, which is 25 cm

Substitute the value of x into the expression for the longest side.

d The width is $x - 1 = 11 - 1$, which is 10 cm.

The area is therefore $25 \times 10 = 250 \text{ cm}^2$

---

a 4 metres

One less than five bricks = 4

b 8 bricks

Length + 1 = number of bricks

c

Any combination of 4 and 3 to total 15.

$4 \text{ m} + 4 \text{ m} + 4 \text{ m} + 3 \text{ m}$

$3 \text{ m} + 3 \text{ m} + 3 \text{ m} + 3 \text{ m} + 3 \text{ m}$

d 19 bricks

20 bricks

$4 \text{ m} + 4 \text{ m} + 4 \text{ m} + 3 \text{ m}$

Would need: $5 + 5 + 5 + 4$ bricks (for every metre of plank there is one extra brick)

or

$3 \text{ m} + 3 \text{ m} + 3 \text{ m} + 3 \text{ m} + 3 \text{ m}$

Would need: $4 + 4 + 4 + 4 + 4$ bricks

3 The diameter of the cherry tree is 3 m. I will assume it has a radius of 1.5 m. This means the tree can be planted anywhere 1.5 m away from the edge of the lawn.

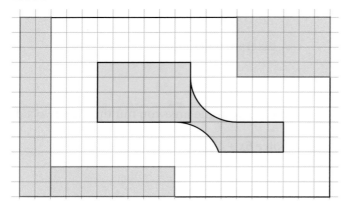

This diagram has a scale of two squares to 1 m. The yellow shaded area is where the cherry tree can be planted.

You can choose any scale you like.

For the cherry tree there are straight lines 1.5 m away from the edge of the lawn and arcs (parts of circles) at the corners of the flower bed and the vegetable patch.

4 The helicopters cover 25 km from each town, so we need two circles. The fire brigade covers the section closer to B than A, so we need the locus of points equidistant from both towns.

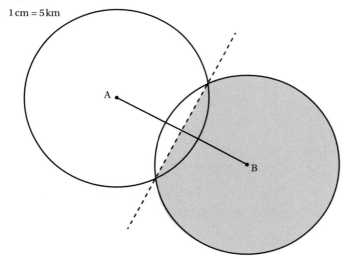

With compasses draw a circle centre B and radius 5 cm.

With compasses draw a circle centre A and radius 5 cm.

The locus of points equidistant from B and A is the perpendicular bisector of line AB.

Shade the region that is closer to B than A and covered by helicopter B.

5

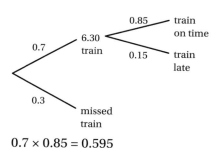

A tree diagram might be useful here.

$0.7 \times 0.85 = 0.595$

---

6 a

+	1	2	3	4	5
1	2	3	4	5	6
2	3	4	5	6	7
3	4	5	6	7	8
4	5	6	7	8	9
5	6	7	8	9	10

Here is a diagram that will work well.

b 10

c $\frac{3}{25}$ (or 0.12)

7

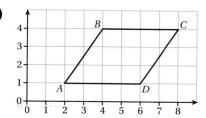

A diagram of the situation helps you see what is going on.

a $\overrightarrow{CD} = \begin{pmatrix} -2 \\ -3 \end{pmatrix}$

b $\overrightarrow{AB} = \begin{pmatrix} 2 \\ 3 \end{pmatrix}$

The length AB is the same as the length CD but the vectors are in opposite directions.

c $ABCD$ is a parallelogram – a four sided shape with two sets of parallel sides.

BC is $\begin{pmatrix} 4 \\ 0 \end{pmatrix}$ and AD is $\begin{pmatrix} 4 \\ 0 \end{pmatrix}$ so BC is parallel to AD

AB is $\begin{pmatrix} 2 \\ 3 \end{pmatrix}$ and DC is $\begin{pmatrix} 2 \\ 3 \end{pmatrix}$ so AB is parallel to DC

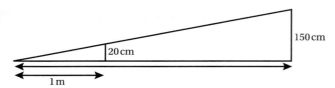

150 cm

20 cm

1 m

A good diagram shows that this is a question about similar triangles.

The scale factor of the enlargement is 150 cm ÷ 20 cm = 7.5.

Make sure the units of length are the same.

1 m × 7.5 = 7.5 m

The projector needs to move back another 6.5 m.

The image needs to be 7.5 larger to fill the screen. This means that the projector needs to be 7.5 times further away.

	Hot chocolate	Tea	Coffee	Total
Women	**8**	9	**12**	29
Men	8	**7**	**10**	**25**
Total	16	**16**	22	54

A diagram like this 2-way table will help here to find who liked what drink and how many workers there were altogether.

Of the 54 workers surveyed, 22 preferred coffee, 16 preferred tea and 16 preferred hot chocolate.

Peter was incorrect. Tea is not the most popular drink, coffee is the most popular hot drink among the workers, and hot chocolate is equally as popular as tea.

Mr Rixon's class

Mrs Lloyd's class

marks

A box plot might be helpful here.

Class	Mean score	Median score	Range	IQR	Lowest score	Highest score
Mr Rixson	7.5	7.5	9	4	3	12
Mrs Lloyd	9	7	17	14.5	1	18

The interquartile range is shown with a dotted line because you cannot be exactly sure where that goes (you don't know the lower quartile or the upper quartile).

The median for both classes is very similar. This tells you that half of Mr Rixson's class got 7.5 or more and half of Mrs Lloyd's class got 7 or more marks. The best person in Mrs Lloyd's class did much better than the best person in Mr Rixson's class.

The mean mark in Mrs Lloyd's class was bigger than the mean mark for Mr Rixson's class, and this, combined with the bigger interquartile range tells you that there must have been several very high scores in Lloyd's class. In fact, the upper quartile for Mrs Lloyd's class must be better than the best score in Mr Rixson's class, which means at least 3 of Mrs Lloyd's students did better than Mr Rixson's best student.

At the bottom end it looks as if at least 3 of Mrs Lloyd's students did worse than Mr Rixson's worst student.

It is difficult to tell, but because the means are different you can probably say that Mrs Lloyd's class did better.

11 **a**

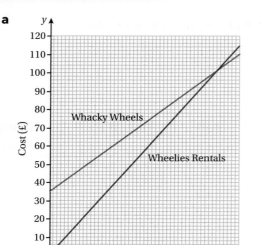

The graph is helpful in answering the rest of this question.

b Wheelies Rentals

Whacky Wheels: £35 + £75 = £110

Wheelies Rentals: £5 + £23 = £115

c yes, she would have saved £5

a

25x + 75 or 50x – 75

There are 25 patches in each row.

The width could be $25(x + 3) = 25x + 75$

or it could be $25(2x - 3) = 50x - 75$

b $64x - 96$ or $32x + 96$

$32(2x - 3)$ or it could be $32(x + 3)$

c The two possible expressions for the area are
$(25x + 75)(64x - 96)$ and $(50x - 75)(32x + 96)$

These are equal because they are both equivalent
to working out $25(x + 3) \times 32(2x - 3)$.

This is $800(2x^2 + 3x - 9)$, which is the same as
$1600x^2 + 2400x - 7200$.

d $2.8\,\text{m}^2$ is the same as $2.8 \times 100\,\text{cm} \times 100\,\text{cm} = 28\,000\,\text{cm}^2$.

The equation is therefore: $1600x^2 + 2400x - 7200 = 28\,000$

Dividing through by 800 gives: $2x^2 + 3x - 9 = 35$

$2x^2 + 3x - 44 = 0$ can be factorised to give $(2x + 11)(x - 4) = 0$, so $x = -5.5$ (which isn't possible for this
scenario) or $x = 4$.

The dimensions of the patches are: $2x - 3$ by $x + 3$
and when $x = 4$ this gives $5\,\text{cm}$ by $7\,\text{cm}$.

13 **a**

Here is a picture of the container.

The volume is $x^2 \times h$. This equals 1440, so:
$x^2h = 1440$, which means $h = \dfrac{1440}{x^2}$

b The base has area x^2. Each of the side walls (shown in yellow on the diagram) has area hx, which simplifies to give $\dfrac{1440}{x}$. There are four of these, so the total area of paper is $x^2 + \dfrac{5760}{x}$

$h = \dfrac{1440}{x^2}$, so $hx = \dfrac{1440x}{x^2} = \dfrac{1440}{x}$

c 12 cm by 12 cm

$1440 = x^2 \times 10$

So $144 = x^2$

$x = \pm12$ (reject the negative option)

d 624 cm^2

14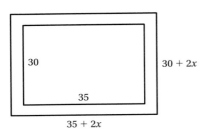

This is the top view of the pool and the path.

30
30 + 2x
35
35 + 2x

a $(35 + 2x)(30 + 2x) - 35 \times 30 = 130x + 4x^2$

You could work out the area of the outer rectangle and then subtract the area of the inner rectangle.

b $3196.80 \div 30 = 106.56$

Square metres of border

$4x^2 + 130x = 106.56$

Use the quadratic formula or completing the square to solve this equation.

$x = 0.8$ m

15

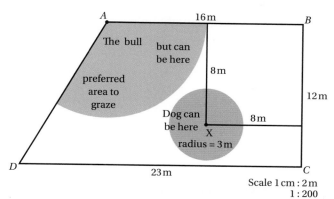

A good way to solve this is to draw a scale diagram. You could use a scale of 1 cm to 2 m.

On the scale diagram, construct:

- a circle of radius 1.5 cm about C to show where the dog can go.

- a locus of radius 4 cm about A between the fence lines DA and AB where the bull can roam.

Any path between D and B that does not enter either of the shaded areas would be safe to use.

16

A probability tree diagram is probably most useful.

$\frac{1}{23}$ Y

$\frac{22}{23}$ W* $\frac{3}{25} \times \frac{2}{24} \times \frac{22}{23} = \frac{132}{13\,800}$

$\frac{2}{24}$ Y

$\frac{22}{23}$

$\frac{2}{23}$ Y * $\frac{3}{25} \times \frac{22}{24} \times \frac{2}{23} = \frac{132}{13\,800}$

$\frac{3}{25}$ Y

$\frac{22}{24}$ W

$\frac{21}{23}$ W

$\frac{2}{23}$ Y * $\frac{22}{25} \times \frac{3}{24} \times \frac{2}{23} = \frac{132}{13\,800}$

$\frac{3}{24}$ Y

$\frac{21}{23}$ W

$\frac{22}{25}$ W

$\frac{21}{24}$ W

$\frac{3}{23}$ Y

$\frac{20}{23}$ W

a $\dfrac{6}{13\,800} = \dfrac{1}{2300}$

b $\dfrac{9240}{13\,800} = \dfrac{77}{115}$

c The three routes labelled on the diagram all work, so you need to add them and will get
$\dfrac{396}{13\,800} = \dfrac{33}{1150}$

17 a
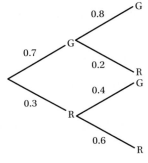

A tree diagram might help.

$0.7 \times 0.8 = 0.56$

The required probability is for two greens.

b $(0.7 \times 0.2) + (0.3 \times 0.4) = 0.26$

Two outcomes: green then red (GR) and red then green (RG).

18

Here is the tree diagram.

badminton   squash

G wins both: 0.85×0.35

0.85 G wins — 0.35 G wins

0.65 R wins — G wins badminton, R wins squash: 0.85×0.65

0.15 R wins — 0.35 G wins — R wins badminton, G wins squash: 0.15×0.35

0.65 R wins — R wins both: 0.15×0.65

a $0.85 \times 0.35 = 0.2975$

b $0.15 \times 0.35 = 0.0525$

c $0.85 \times 0.65 + 0.15 \times 0.35 = 0.605$

19
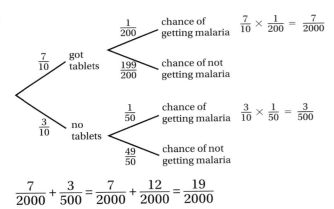

$\dfrac{7}{2000} + \dfrac{3}{500} = \dfrac{7}{2000} + \dfrac{12}{2000} = \dfrac{19}{2000}$

20 **a**

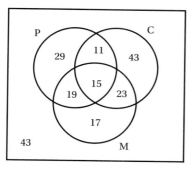

A Venn diagram is likely to be useful here.

53 study two subjects – so 11 study Physics and Chemistry but not Maths.

74 study Physics, so 15 study all three.

92 study Chemistry, so 43 study only Chemistry.

There are 200 students so 17 study only Maths

b $\dfrac{17}{200}$

c $\dfrac{68}{200} = \dfrac{17}{50}$

11 studied Chemistry and Physics, 19 studied Physics and Maths, 23 studied Chemistry and Maths, 15 studied all three.

Total 68 of 200 students.

21 **a**

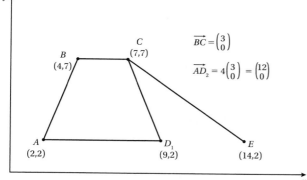

$\overrightarrow{BC} = \begin{pmatrix} 3 \\ 0 \end{pmatrix}$

$\overrightarrow{AD_2} = 4\begin{pmatrix} 3 \\ 0 \end{pmatrix} = \begin{pmatrix} 12 \\ 0 \end{pmatrix}$

An isosceles trapezium has one line of symmetry, so D could be (9, 2) as C to D will be 2 units to the right and 5 units downwards.

$D(9, 2)$

The alternative position of D is $(4\frac{5}{29}, \frac{-2}{29})$

b $\overrightarrow{AC} = \begin{pmatrix} 5 \\ 5 \end{pmatrix}$

c $E(14, 2)$

d $\overrightarrow{BE} = \begin{pmatrix} 10 \\ -5 \end{pmatrix}$

22

The ratio of object : distance is the same for both mum and the hill.

$0.12 : 3$

$h : 2000$

$0.12 \div 3 \times 2000 = 80 \, \text{m}$

The hill is about 80 m tall.

> Divide by 3 and multiply by 2000.

> You are not given Eve's height so this is how much taller than Eve the hill is.

23

a width : length

$40 : 55$

$8 : 11$

$112 \div 8 = 14$

$11 \times 14 = 154 \, \text{cm}$

> You may want to draw diagrams to show what is going on.

> This is the length.

b $148.5 \div 11 = 13.5$

$13.5 \times 8 = 108 \, \text{cm}$

> This is the width.

c Width of photo = area ÷ length

$= 127.5 \div 15$

$= 8.5 \, \text{cm}$

Factor of enlargement

= new width ÷ original width

$= 25.5 \div 8.5$

$= 3$

The area will increase by a factor of $3^2 = 9$.

Area of poster $= 127.5 \times 9 \, \text{cm}^2$

$= 1147.5 \, \text{cm}^2$

> First work out the width of the original photo using the length and area given in the question.

> Then work out the scale factor of the enlargement by comparing the two widths.

a i, ii

There are three possible triangles that fit Harriet's description.

iii She could say that the hypotenuse is 5 cm. Other answers are possible too.

For only one triangle to be possible, Harriet must make sure that her conditions follow one of the conditions of congruence:

SSS, SAS, ASA, AAS or RHS

b i

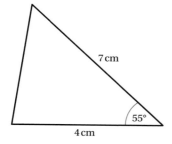

There is only one triangle that satisfies Janet's conditions because she has given SAS.

ii A scale drawing will enable you to measure the length of the third side as 5.7 cm to the nearest mm.

$a^2 = b^2 + c^2 - 2bc\cos A$

$a^2 = 7^2 + 4^2 - 2 \times 7 \times 4 \times \cos 55$

$a = 5.734... \text{ cm}$

A more accurate method to find the length of the third side is to use the cosine rule.

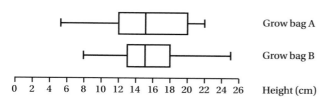

Box plots are useful diagrams to use here.

a Grow bag A: The tomato plants vary quite a lot in height from 5 cm to 22 cm. The middle 50% shows a range of 8cm. The smallest plants are in bag A.

Grow bag B: the tomato plants are more consistent in size with a smaller IQR, although the biggest plant is in bag B.

b Because Elspeth is hoping to sell the tomato plants, she should use Grow bag B so most plants would be around the same size.

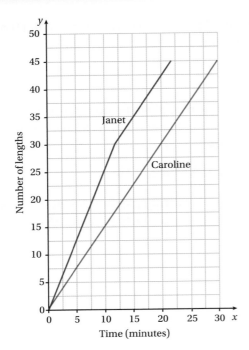

a 15

b 10 minutes

c 45 ÷ 30 = 1.5 lengths per minute

d 8 minutes

e 2 lengths per minute

f 15 more lengths, which is 60 in total, but she might
   get tired and start to slow down.

This is the sort of question where a graph can
really help.

27 a

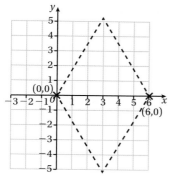

$a^2 + b^2 = c^2$

$3^2 + b^2 = 6^2$

$9 + b^2 = 36$

$b^2 = 27$

$b = \sqrt{27} \ (== 5.196...)$

$(3, \sqrt{27})$

$(3, -\sqrt{27})$

There are two possible locations for the third vertex.

The x-coordinate of the midpoint of the base is 3.

Use Pythagoras' theorem to calculate the vertical height of the equilateral triangle.

b

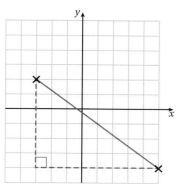

Here is a diagram showing the two points.

This time you only need to know the length of the sides. Pythagoras tells you the side has a length of 10.

$6^2 + 8^2 = c^2$

$c^2 = 100$

$c = \sqrt{100} = 10$

Now, if you have an equilateral triangle of side 10:

$5^2 + b^2 = 10^2$

$25 + b^2 = 100$

$b^2 = 75$

$b = \sqrt{75} \ (= 8.660...)$

$\text{Area} = \frac{1}{2} \times 10 \times \sqrt{75}$

$\text{Area} = 43.301...$

43.3 square units

Use Pythagoras' theorem again to find the vertical height.

Calculate the area of the equilateral triangle ($\frac{1}{2} \times$ base $\times$ height)

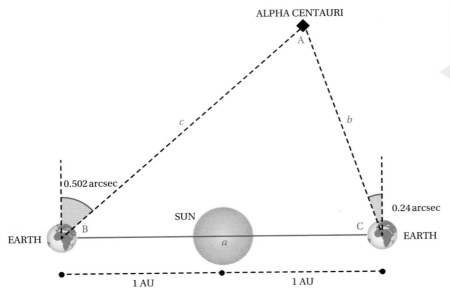

There are lots of aspects of this question that aren't particularly clear, so you will need to make some assumptions (which is fine as long as you explain them) and a good diagram will be a very important starting point.

It looks as if the angles are measured perpendicularly from the line through the Sun, so:

angle B is $90° - 0.502$ arcsec

angle $C = 90° - 0.24$ arcsec

angle A is $0.502 + 0.24 = 0.742$ arcsec

$$\frac{a}{\sin A} = \frac{b}{\sin B} = \frac{c}{\sin C}$$

$$b = \frac{2\text{AU}}{\sin(0.742\text{arcsec})} \times \sin(90° - 0.502\text{arcsec})$$

This gives $b = 8.33955 \times 10^{13}$

$$c = \frac{2\text{AU}}{\sin(0.742\text{arcsec})} \times \sin(90° - 0.24\text{arcsec})$$

This gives $c = 8.33955 \times 10^{13}$

The distance is therefore about 8.3×10^{13} km

It is not obvious which distance is being asked for so let's work out lengths b and c.

These answers are the same for the first 10 significant figures (which makes sense because Alpha Centauri is very, very far away compared to the diameter of the orbit of the Earth).

29 **a** A then B then C

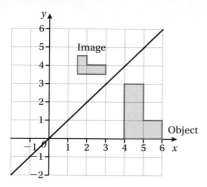

Choose a shape without any symmetry to easily see what is going on.

C then B then A

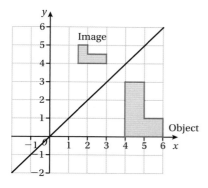

The orientation and size of the final image are the same when the transformations are carried out in a different order, but it ends up in a different place.

b 6

A, B, C

A, C, B

B, A, C

B, C, A

C, A, B

C, B, A

Consider all the possible arrangements of the three transformations.

You have already drawn the first and last one.

The others result in an image that is the same size and same way around, but which are in a different place.

1 But you do know that $\sqrt{64} = 8$ and $\sqrt{81} = 9$, so $8 < \sqrt{70} < 9$

You don't know how big $\sqrt{70}$ is.

Looking at the statement in the question:

$10\sqrt{70} > 8 \times 10$ so the statement is incorrect.

2 $835 \div 16.5 = 50.60$

If the figures were exact then you would work out $840 \div 16$. Here, to be safe, you need to assume the van can only cope with 835 kg (its lower limit) and that the stones weigh 16.5 kg (their upper limit).

He can transport 50 stones.

3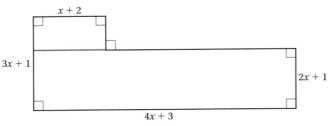

You can't work out the area of the shape immediately, but you can work it out by working out separately the area of the rectangles in it. There are several ways to divide up the shape. The diagram shows one.

a The area is $x(x + 2) + (2x + 1)(4x + 3)$

$9x^2 + 12x + 3$

b $x = 5$

c $9 \times 5^2 + 12 \times 5 + 3 = 288\,\text{m}^2$

d The perimeter $= 14x + 8$. When $x = 5$ the perimeter is $14 \times 5 + 8 = 78\,\text{m}$

The start post will be the end post so 78 posts are needed.

e $78 \times 3 = 234\,\text{m}$ of wire

f $78 \times 18.5 + 234 \times 2.30 = £1981.20$

4

You might not be able to answer this immediately, but you can make some simultaneous equations and solve them.

6 mangoes and 4 pawpaws cost £5.80.

Use the first sentence and double the amounts.

5 mangoes and 4 pawpaws cost £5.50, so the extra mango must cost 30p.

Use the second sentence. The number of pawpaws is the same in both statements, so you can use this to work out the cost of a mango.

The price of a pawpaw is £1.

5 **a**

The area of the triangular cross-section is $\frac{1}{2} \times 6 \times 8$
$= 24\,\text{cm}^2$

The volume of the prism if $24 \times 9 = 216\,\text{cm}^3$

b The volume of the pentagonal prism is $36 \times L = 216$

$L = 216 \div 36 = 6\,\text{cm}$

6

Volume of cylinder $= \pi \times 3^2 \times 11 = 311.01767\ldots\,\text{cm}^3$

> You could start by working out the volume of a cylinder of water that is 11 cm high.

> Volume of water (a cylinder) = area of circular base × height

$311\,\text{cm}^3 = 311\,\text{ml}$

> Volume of water (in ml)

$500\,\text{ml} - 311.01767\,\text{ml} = 189\,\text{ml}$ (3 s.f.)

> Volume of water left in bottle

---

7 **a** 3 : 5 gives 8 parts.

> Start by working out the number of parts in the ratio.

$32 \div 8 = 4$

$3 \times 4 = 12$ non-calculator questions on each test.
$5 \times 4 = 20$ calculator questions.

b 15 tests $\times$ 20 = 300 calculator questions

c $15 \times 32 = 480$ questions, so each teacher will write 240 questions.

> This is complicated, so let's find out how many questions there are altogether.

60 of those are calculator questions and 180 are non-calculator.

$\frac{60}{240} = \frac{1}{4}$

---

8 **a** You know that p(green ball) = 0.64,
so p(not a green ball) = 0.36

> You can't solve this immediately, but you do know this.

The probability of getting a white ball is the same as that of getting a yellow ball, so they must each be
$0.36 \div 2 = 0.18$.

b 9 yellow balls out of the total number = 0.18

$0.18 = \frac{18}{100} = \frac{9}{50}$ so there are 50 balls in total.

9   The probability that Sharon or Frances finish first is
0.23 + 0.15 = 0.38

So the probability Sue or Anisha finish first is 1 – 0.38
= 0.62

10

Student	Cumulative number of sixes	Relative frequency
A	7	0.7
B	11	0.55
C	14	0.47
D	20	0.5
E	24	0.48

It probably makes sense to start working out the probability after each student has had a go.

Now you might want to skip a few. After 10 students have done their throws, there are 44 sixes and the relative frequency is 0.44.

After 15 students have taken their throws, there are 68 sixes and the relative frequency is 0.45.

After 20 students have taken their throws, there are 83 sixes and the relative frequency is 0.415.

The relative frequency is going up and down, but it looks as if it is settling somewhere close to 0.4.

When more trials happen the relative frequency is generally closer to the actual value.

The theoretical probability for a fair dice is $\frac{1}{6} = 0.17$

The actual value of the probability is probably about 0.4, which means that the dice is a biased one.

---

11   12 × 5 = 60

This is a challenging problem.

If the mean of 5 numbers is 12, what do you know? When you work out the mean of five numbers you add them up and divide by 5, so before the sum was divided by 5 it must have totalled 60 (because 60 ÷ 5 = 12).

60 ÷ 4 = 15

You also know that there are 15 parts in the ratio.

4 : 4 : 12 : 16 : 24
The largest numbers is 24

Multiplying the numbers in the ratio by 4 gives these figures, and the largest one is 24.

a $40 \times 30 = 1200$ square units

Start by working out the area of the rectangle.

$\frac{4}{5}$ of $1200 = 960$

Now you can work out the shaded area.

You want to have $\frac{5}{6}$ of $1200 = 1000$ shaded, so you need to shade an extra 40 square units.

b 960 is shaded from the first rectangle.

$\frac{2}{3}$ of $1200 = 800$ is shaded from the second rectangle.

One way to do this is to work out the total area and the total amount that is shaded.

The fraction of the whole thing that is shaded is:

$$\frac{960 + 800}{1200 + 1200} = \frac{1760}{2400} = \frac{11}{15}$$

c $\frac{3}{4}$ of $2400 = 1800$, so an extra 40 square units need to be shaded.

You already know that 1760 square units are shaded.

 $6 \div 0.5 = 12$

$6 \div 0 = $ Error

There is a link between $20 \div 4 = 5$ and $4 \times 5 = 20$.

There are lots of ways to explain why. Here is one.

$6 \div 0.5 = x$ means that $0.5 \times x = 6$

This makes is clear that $x = 12$

$6 \div 0 = y$ means that $0 \times y = 6$

It is not possible to multiply 0 by something and to get the answer of 6, so $6 \div 0$ does not have an answer.

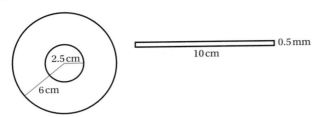

The diagrams show the end of the roll of paper and the side view of a single piece of paper.

$\pi \times 6^2 - \pi \times 2.5^2 = 93.46238\,\text{cm}^2$

The width of the paper is irrelevant. You only need to worry about the area of the end of the roll.

The area of the 'ring'

$10 \times 0.05 = 0.5\,\text{cm}^2$

The area of the side of one piece of paper.

Convert 0.5 mm into 0.05 cm

$93.46238 \div 0.5 = 186.92476$

Work out how many pieces of paper have the same area as the ring.

This means there are approximately 187 sheets on the roll. You cannot tell whether this is exact because the sheets might be compressed when they are rolled up. If there are 200 sheets then they must be slightly thinner, so they are not as high quality as was claimed.

You can't immediately work out the size (using numbers) of the sides of the rectangle, but you know that the area of the rectangle is the same as the area of the square, so start by working those out.

The area of the rectangle is $(x + 1)(x + 11)$
$= x^2 + 12x + 11$
The area of the square is $(x + 5)^2 = x^2 + 10x + 25$
These are equal, so $x^2 + 12x + 11 = x^2 + 10x + 25$
This simplifies to give $2x = 14$, so $x = 7$
The dimensions of the rectangle are therefore 8 cm by 18 cm
$18 \times 8 = 144\,\text{cm}^2$

a The big square has area $5x \times 5x = 25x^2$

Subtract the area of the small square (x^2) to leave $24x^2$

b $24x^2 = 1944$, so $x^2 = 81$, which means that here $x = 9$

You can't immediately see what the perimeter will be, so start by working out the value of x.

The perimeter of the shape is $20x$, which equals 180 cm.

a The angles in a regular hexagon are 120°, and those in a regular pentagon are 108°.

> In a regular shape all the angles must be the same so working these out might be a good starting point.

The angles around a point should add up to 360°, but here they make 336°, so they don't fit the pattern of the quilt.

b 3 × 120° = 360°, so regular hexagons will fit around the edge. Equilateral triangles would also fit:

c A regular decagon can be surrounded by regular pentagons.

> The interior angle of a regular pentagon is 108°.

> So two regular pentagons have angles of 108 + 108 = 216°. This leaves 360° – 216° = 144°
>
> You now have to identify the regular polygon that has an interior angle of 144°.
>
> The exterior angle is 180 – 144 = 36
>
> Exterior angles always sum to 360°, so there must be 10 of them and the shape must have 10 sides.

18

Because of the way the paper has been folded you know the marked angle is 45°.

360° ÷ 45° = 8, so 8 of the kites will fit together.

19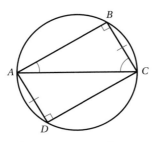

$A\hat{B}C = 90°$ and $A\hat{D}C = 90°$

Because the angle in a semicircle is a right angle.

$A\hat{B}C = A\hat{D}C$

Compare triangles *ABC* and *CDA*.

$AD = BC$

AC is common to both triangles and is the hypotenuse.

So, by RHS, triangles *ABC* and *CDA* are congruent.

This means $B\hat{A}C = A\hat{C}D$. But $B\hat{A}C + A\hat{C}B = 90°$, so $D\hat{C}B = 90°$

For a similar reason, $D\hat{A}B = 90°$

All four angles in the quadrilateral *ABCD* are 90°, so it is a rectangle.

20 **a**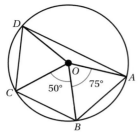

$O\hat{C}B = O\hat{B}C = (180° - 50°) \div 2 = 65°$

You need to show which angles you are looking at, so first draw in lines from each vertex of the trapezium to the centre of the circle and label the angles given in the question.

$O\hat{A}B = O\hat{B}A = (180° - 75°) \div 2 = 52.5°$

Each of the four triangles is isosceles (because the lines OA, OB, OC are radii).

Use this to calculate the other angles in triangles BOC and AOB.

$C\hat{B}A = 65° + 52.5° = 117.5°$
$B\hat{A}D = 180° - 117.5° = 62.5°$

Because AD is parallel to CB (trapezium), DAB + ABC = 180° (supplementary).

$O\hat{A}D = O\hat{D}A = 62.5° - 52.5° = 10°$

Now calculate OÂD in the isosceles triangle OAD.

$A\hat{O}D = 180° - 20° = 160°$

Now calculate AÔD, remembering to subtract both OÂD, OD̂A

$C\hat{O}D = 360° - 50° - 75° - 160° = 75°$

Angles around a point sum to 360°

b OA = OB = OC = OD because they are all the radius of the circle, and so by SAS triangle COD is congruent to triangle AOB. This means CD is equal to AB, so ABCD is an isosceles trapezium.

21

θ	$\sin \theta$	$\cos \theta$	$\sin \theta \div \cos \theta$
0°	0	1	0
30°	$\frac{1}{2}$	$\frac{\sqrt{3}}{2}$	$\frac{1}{2} \div \frac{\sqrt{3}}{2} = \frac{1}{2} \times \frac{2}{\sqrt{3}} = \frac{1}{\sqrt{3}}$
45°	$\frac{\sqrt{2}}{2}$	$\frac{\sqrt{2}}{2}$	1
60°	$\frac{\sqrt{3}}{2}$	$\frac{1}{2}$	$\frac{\sqrt{3}}{2} \div \frac{1}{2} = \frac{\sqrt{3}}{2} \times \frac{2}{1} = \sqrt{3}$
90°	1	0	1 ÷ 0, which is undefined

It seems sensible to start by following the instructions and filling in the missing boxes in the table.

The values in the final column do look like tan θ.

In a right-angled triangle: $\sin \theta = \dfrac{\text{opp}}{\text{hyp}}$ and $\cos \theta = \dfrac{\text{adj}}{\text{hyp}}$

This means that

$\dfrac{\sin \theta}{\cos \theta} = \dfrac{\text{opp}}{\text{hyp}} \div \dfrac{\text{adj}}{\text{hyp}} = \dfrac{\text{opp}}{\text{hyp}} \times \dfrac{\text{hyp}}{\text{adj}} = \dfrac{\text{opp}}{\text{adj}}$

$\dfrac{\text{opp}}{\text{adj}} = \tan \theta$,

so it is the case that $\sin \theta \div \cos \theta = \tan \theta$

22 $\frac{2}{16}$ had a dot, which is $\frac{1}{8}$.

That means the 16 he caught were about $\frac{1}{8}$ of the population, so there are 16 × 8 = 128 altogether, which is below the limit of 150.

As long as the woodlice he marked had mixed themselves up with the others, the fraction with the number he captured originally is the same fraction of the whole population as the fraction with dots he recaptured.

 23 **a**

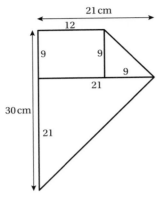

Draw a good diagram and then work out the lengths of the sides.

Rectangle: 12 × 9 = 108

Small triangle: $\frac{1}{2}$ × 9 × 9 = 40.5

Large triangle: $\frac{1}{2}$ × 21 × 21 = 220.5

Now there is enough information to work out the areas.

Either work out the area of the rectangle and the two triangles and add them, or work out the area of the original sheet of paper and subtract two triangles.

Total area = 369 cm^2

b Area of the original sheet is 21 × 30 = 630 cm^2

The fraction is $\frac{369}{630} = \frac{41}{70}$

Start with a labelled diagram of the hat.

Circumference of the base is $\pi \times 2r = 18\pi$, and when the hat is unrolled, this is the length of the arc.

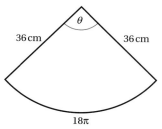

This is a sector of a circle.

The radius of the sector = 36 cm, so the circumference of a full circle would be $72\,\pi$.

The arc is $18\,\pi$, which is $\frac{1}{4}$ of the circumference, so the angle is $\frac{1}{4}$ of $360° = 90°$

Hence the sector required will be a quarter of a circle of radius 36 cm.

This will fit on a square of side 36 cm.

  Radius = 16 cm ÷ 2 = 8 cm

Volume = $2 \times \pi \times 8^3 \div 3 = 1072.93$ cm³ (2 d.p.)

Radius = 11 cm ÷ 2 = 5.5 cm

Volume of large bowl (hemisphere) = $2\pi r^3 \div 3$

$2 \times \pi \times 5.5$ cm³ $\div 3 = 348.45$ cm³ (2 d.p.)

Volume of small bowl

1072.33 cm³ $- 349.45$ cm³ $= 723.88$ cm³ (2 d.p.)

Difference between volumes of larger and smaller bowls

723.98 ml ÷ 100 = 7.2388

$7.2388 \times 59 = 427$ kcal saved (to the nearest kcal).

Number of kcal in 723.88 ml of soup.

26 Draw the pentagon in and then look at the diagram. To show that the outer pentagon is regular you need to show that the angles are all equal and that the sides are all the same length.

In the original pentagon all the angles were 108° (angles in a regular pentagon) and in the equilateral triangles the angles are all 60°.

There are lots of ways to explain this.

Start with the angles.

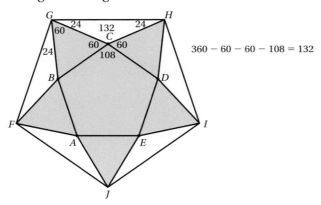

$360 - 60 - 60 - 108 = 132$

The angles in the isosceles triangles around the edge are therefore 132, 24, 24.

The angles in the outer pentagon are therefore 24 + 60 + 24 = 108°, which are the angles for a regular pentagon.

All the sides of the original pentagon are equal (because it is regular), so the equilateral triangles are all congruent. The isosceles triangles are all congruent (by SAS) so the sides of the outer pentagon are all the same.

Because the sides are all equal and the angles are equal the outer pentagon is regular.

27   1 minute = 60 s

1 hour = 60 minutes = 60 × 60 s = 3600 s

1 day = 24 hours = 24 × 3600 s = 86 300 s

1 year = 365 days = 365 × 84 400 s = 315 360 00s

First calculate the number of km in a light year (ly).

To do this, calculate the number of seconds in 1 year.

2.99×10^5 km/s × 315 360 00 s = $9.429... \times 10^{12}$ km

Now calculate the number of km travelled by light in one year.

$4.22 \times 9.429... \times 10^{12}$ km = $3.979... \times 10^{13}$ km

Convert 4.22 ly into km.

$3.979... \times 10^{13}$ km = $3.979... \times 10^{16}$ m.

Convert this into metres

$3.979... \times \dfrac{10^{16} \text{ m}}{400 \text{ m}} = 9.947... \times 10^{13}$

Calculate the number of laps of a 400 m track that are required to cover this distance.

You would need to run approximately 10×10^{13} or 1×10^{14} or 100 000 000 000 000 laps of a standard 400 m running track to cover the distance from Earth to Proxima Centuri.

 28

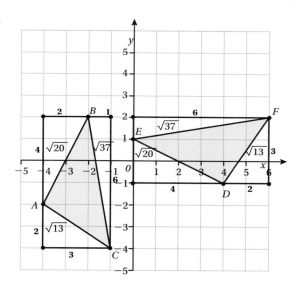

Draw an accurate version of the diagram on a grid.

Then work out the length of each of the sides, using Pythagoras' theorem.

The two triangles have identical sides, so by SSS they are congruent.

50 m

40 m

It seems sensible to work out the distances the two animals travel.

The tortoise travels $\sqrt{40^2 + 50^2} = \sqrt{4100}$

The hare travels $40 + 50 = 90$

You know how fast the tortoise moves, so you can work out how long it takes the tortoise to complete the race

$$\text{Time} = \frac{\sqrt{4100}}{0.1} = 640.312\,\text{s}$$

Time = distance ÷ speed

The hare only needs to travel 90m in 640.312 seconds, so the lowest speed it can go at and still beat the tortoise is $\dfrac{90}{640.312} = 0.1406\,\text{m/s}$

1

This diagram has extra lines on it.

It shows that $\frac{9}{16}$ of the diagram is purple.

Team **A** have given an area rather than a proportion.
0 marks

Team **B** have got the wrong fraction. Maybe they saw that $\frac{3}{4}$ of this part was shaded:

But that is not the whole thing.
0 or 1 mark

Team **C** are correct. Maybe they used the idea that the inner big white triangle is not included (leaving $\frac{3}{4}$ of the whole diagram) and then $\frac{3}{4}$ of that is shaded, which is $\frac{3}{4} \times \frac{3}{4}$. This equals $\frac{9}{16}$.
4 marks

Team **D** are correct. $\frac{8}{6} = 0.5625$.
4 marks

2 **a**

The length of the fence is:

$\pi \times 17 = 53.407\,075\ldots$ m

53.4 m

b

semicircle with
diameter of 10 m

Length of fence:

21.5 + 10 + 21.5 + semicircle with diameter of 10 m

Semicircle:

$\pi \times 10 \div 2$

Total length is 68.7 m

68.7 m – 53.4 m = 15.3 m

Ian will need to buy 15.3 m more fencing than
Gerry.

A copy of the diagram with the extra line added
will help.

Circumference of circle = π × diameter

Round the answer to 3 s.f.

Calculate the difference in lengths of fencing.

Conclusion.

3

650 m

130 m

a

a

130 m

650 m

Add some lines to make it into a rectangle.

This makes it easy to see that the perimeter of the
shape (which is the same as the perimeter of the
rectangle) is $a + a + 650 + 650 = 2a + 1300$

This is the same as 2.28 km, so (after converting that to
2280 m) you can make an equation:

$2a + 1300 = 2280$

Solving this gives $a = 490$ m, so the value of a required
is 0.49 km.

Make sure you answer in the units asked for.

4

Approach 1:

The interior angle of an octagon = 135°

135° ÷ 2 = 67.5°

$67.5° + 67.5° + a = 180°$

$a = 180° - 135° = 45°$

Approach 2:

Making a copy of the half-octagons and rotating it creates two octagons. The angle a is the exterior angle.

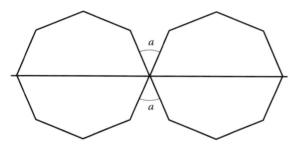

Exterior angle of an octagon = 360° ÷ 8 = 45°

There are several other ways to approach this problem.

The octagon has been cut in half so the angles adjacent to the one labelled a will each be half of the interior angle of the octagon.

The sum of angles on a straight line is 180°.

5 **a**

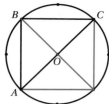

The inner shape is a square, so the angle *ABC* is 90°

Here are some changes to the diagram that make it easier to see what is going on.

b

The extra lines show that there are 8 equal angles around the centre of the circle.

Each angle is therefore 360° ÷ 8 = 45°

Triangle *OCB* is isosceles, which means angles *B* and *C* are equal and add up to 135°. Each one is therefore 67.5°.

Triangle *OAB* is also isosceles and the angle *AOB* = 135° (three lots of 45°). Angles *A* and *B* are equal and add up to 45°, so each one is 22.5°.

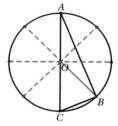

Angle *ABC* is 67.5° + 22.5° = 90°

c

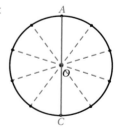

This will show that the angle at *B* is 90°, as in part **b**. Angles *BAC* and *BCA* are the other two angles and must sum to 90° since the angles in a triangle sum to 180°.

The angles around the centre are all 36° (360° ÷ 10). When you choose a point for *B* you will make isosceles triangles and can work out the other angles as in part **b**.

6 A good extra line to try is one from the centre of the circle to the tangent point (because this does some special things, like forming right angles).

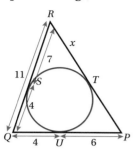

The sides of the triangle are all tangents to the circle.

$SQ = UQ$, so $SQ = 4$.

RS is equal to RT, so $x = 7$.

You know this because two tangents from the same point are the same length.

7

Divide the area into congruent shapes. Congruent shapes have the same area, so you could start by working out the area of the original diagram, which is 12 square units.

a

To have three congruent shapes the area of each one must be 4 square units. An easy way to make an area of 4 is to have a square.

b

To make four congruent shapes the area of each one must be 3 square units. If you try to use straight lines it doesn't work, either with rectangles or with triangles. There are other shapes that have an area of 3 square units, and these will work here.

8 **a** 3.6 m = 360 cm

360 cm ÷ 18 cm = 20 stairs in the staircase.

The stairs must cover a vertical distance of 3.6 m. Each step is 18 cm high.

b Base length of staircase = 20 × 28 cm = 560 cm

$a^2 + b^2 = c^2$

$560^2 + 360^2 = c^2$

$443\,200 = c^2$

$c = 665.73...$ cm

The banister rail will go diagonally up the stairs. It will need to be the same length as the diagonal length of the staircase. Use Pythagoras' theorem to calculate this.

The banister rail will need to be 6.66 m in length (to the nearest cm).

9 **a** The top is $6 - x$

The perimeter is 12, so the top and the side together add up to 6.

The area is therefore $(6 - x)x$, which can also be written as $6x - x^2$

b The area is equal to 6.3m², so you get the equation (using the area expression from part **a**):

$6x - x^2 = 6.3$

The area of the tablecloth (2.2 × 3.1 = 6.82 m²) is big enough, but it might not be the right dimensions to fit neatly on the table, so you need to work out the dimensions of the table.

$10x^2 - 60x + 63 = 0$

Rearrange and multiply through by 10.

$x = 4.64$ or $x = 1.36$

Use the quadratic formula.

These are the dimensions of the table (because $6 - 4.64 = 1.36$).

The tablecloth won't fit.

10

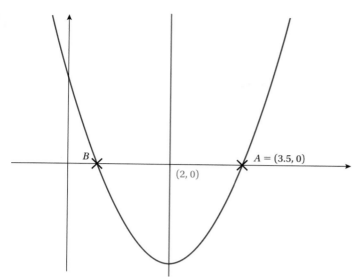

The question states that the graph is symmetrical about the line $x = 2$, so it makes sense to draw that line on a copy of the graph.

The coordinates of point B are (0.5, 0).

Now you can see that the crossing value for point A is 1.5 to the right of the line of reflection, so point B must cross at 1.5 to the left of the line.

C is (3.5, 0) and D is (0.5, 0).

In the second diagram the quadratic has been reflected in the x-axis so the crossing points are the same.

11 **a**

The red lines on the diagram show that you need 180° plus a third of 180° (60°), which is 240° in total.

b When the minute hand makes a full turn the hour hand moves one hour, which means the hour hand moves at $\frac{1}{12}$ of the speed.

$\frac{1}{12}$ of 240° = 20°

12 If Z, S and P are colinear then $\overrightarrow{SP}$ is parallel to $\overrightarrow{ZS}$ and they are multiples of each other.

$$\overrightarrow{SP} = 2u + 3v$$

$$\overrightarrow{ZS} = \frac{1}{2}u + 2v$$

$$4\overrightarrow{ZS} = 2u + 8v$$

There is no way to express $\overrightarrow{SZ}$ as a multiple of $\overrightarrow{SP}$.

Hence Z, S and P are not colinear.

It is worth adding these extra lines to the diagram.

13 a

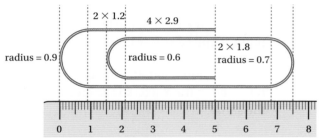

Cut the diagram up into sections and label them.

Curved length = πr

Work out the perimeter of a semicircle.

The straight parts add up to 17.6:

$0.9\pi + 0.6\pi + 0.7\pi = 2.2\pi$

The total length is 24.5 cm (1 d.p.)

Sum the parts to obtain the total length.

b

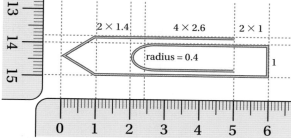

The diagonal parts are the hypotenuse because of a right-angled triangle.

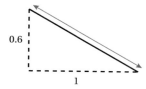

$h = \sqrt{1^2 + 0.6^2}$

The total length of wire is 19.8 cm (1 d.p.), which means the first paperclip contains more wire.

Find the lengths of the sections and sum them.

14 **a**

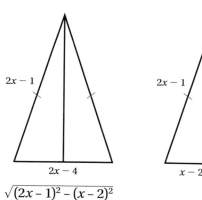

$\sqrt{(2x-1)^2 - (x-2)^2}$

This simplifies to give $\sqrt{3x^2 - 3}$

Put in the extra line; this makes two right-angled triangles.

b $\sqrt{3x^2 - 3} = 12$

$3x^2 - 3 = 144$, so $x = 7$

The base of the original triangle is 10, so the area is 60 cm²

Work out the height of the triangle, using Pythagoras' theorem

You are told the height is 12.

15 **a**

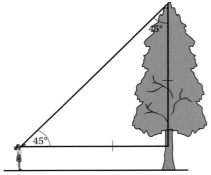

If they are looking up at an angle of 45°, then they create a right-angled, isosceles triangle. (Isosceles because if one angle is 90° and another is 45° then the remaining angle will also be 45°.)

Assuming that the student's height is small compared to the height of the tree, then the horizontal distance along the ground is approximately the same as the height of the tree (two equal sides in an isosceles triangle).

A good diagram will help.

b

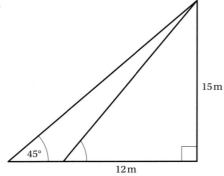

Opposite side = height of tree = 15 m

Adjacent side = 12 m

Guy's angle = $\tan^{-1}\dfrac{15}{12}$ = 51.34...°

Guy's angle is approximately 51°.

16

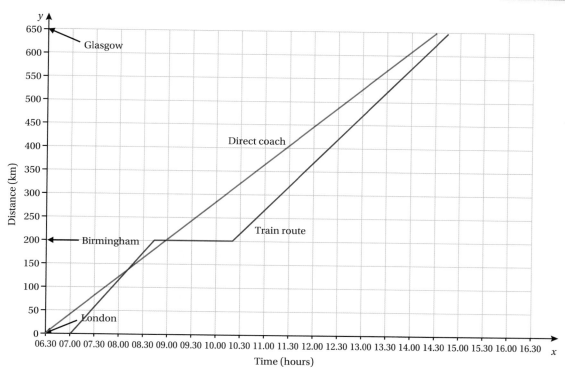

Even though the question doesn't ask you to draw a graph, it is helpful to draw one. Note that the graph shows 'average speeds' as the actual speeds will vary during the journeys.

a $\dfrac{650}{8} = 81.25$ km/h

b 7 h 40 min is $7\dfrac{2}{3}$ h

$650 \div 7\dfrac{2}{3} = 84.8$ km/h

17 The diagram, with its extra lines, shows that 3 straight lines (each $4r$ in length) and 3 arcs, are needed. The 3 arcs together make a circle, so the total length is $12 \times r + 2\pi r$.

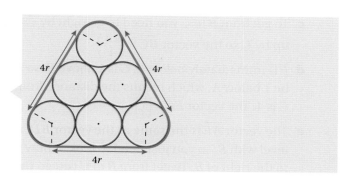

The radius is 2.7 cm, so the length is 49.36 cm.

18

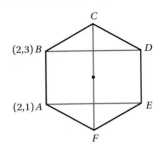

A well-labelled diagram might help.

a $\overrightarrow{DE}$ is the same vector as $\overrightarrow{BA}$. This is $\begin{pmatrix} 0 \\ -2 \end{pmatrix}$ (the same numbers as $\overrightarrow{AB}$ but with the opposite sign).

b

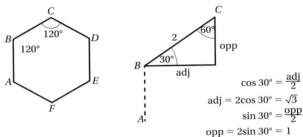

$$\cos 30° = \frac{adj}{2}$$
$$adj = 2\cos 30° = \sqrt{3}$$
$$\sin 30° = \frac{opp}{2}$$
$$opp = 2\sin 30° = 1$$

In a regular hexagon the interior angles are each 120°.

By drawing a right-angled triangle where the hypotenuse side is, you can use the edge of the hexagon (of length 2 units) and trigonometry to calculate the other lengths. of length 2 units

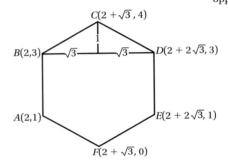

$(2 + \sqrt{3}, 4)$

c To get from B to C you need to go right by $\sqrt{3}$ and up by 1, so the vector $\overrightarrow{BC} = \begin{pmatrix} \sqrt{3} \\ 1 \end{pmatrix}$

d F is immediately below C. C is 1 above B, so F must be 1 below A, which means the distance from F to C is 4. The vector $\overrightarrow{FC} = \begin{pmatrix} 0 \\ 4 \end{pmatrix}$.

e The vector $\overrightarrow{AE}$ is the same as the vector $\overrightarrow{BD}$. D is level with B, so you just need to look at how far D is to the right of B. To get from B to C you go right by $\sqrt{3}$, so you need to double this. The vector $\overrightarrow{AE} = 2\begin{pmatrix} \sqrt{3} \\ 0 \end{pmatrix} = \begin{pmatrix} 2\sqrt{3} \\ 0 \end{pmatrix}$

f The vector $\overrightarrow{AC}$ is the same as $\overrightarrow{AB} + \overrightarrow{BC}$. This is $\begin{pmatrix} 0 \\ 2 \end{pmatrix} + \begin{pmatrix} \sqrt{3} \\ 1 \end{pmatrix} = \begin{pmatrix} \sqrt{3} \\ 3 \end{pmatrix}$

g $\overrightarrow{EF}$ is the same vector as $\overrightarrow{CB}$. This is $\begin{pmatrix} -\sqrt{3} \\ -1 \end{pmatrix}$ (the same numbers as $\overrightarrow{BC}$ but with the opposite sign).

19 **a**

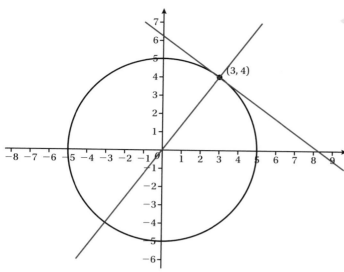

Add some extra lines to help.

The equation of the line passing through $(0,0)$ is
$y = \frac{4}{3}x$

This means the equation of the tangent has a
gradient of $-\frac{3}{4}$

$y = -\frac{3}{4}x$ passes through the point $(3, 4)$. Substituting
in those values gives: $4 = -\frac{3}{4} \times 3 + c$, which
rearranges to give $c = \frac{25}{4}$, which is $6\frac{1}{4}$

This means the equation of the tangent is
$y = -\frac{3}{4}x + 6\frac{1}{4}$

The extra lines show that you have the radius
and the tangent, so the gradients of the two lines
multiply together to give -1.

b

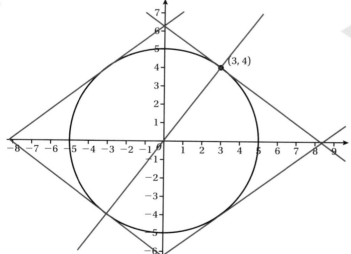

There are lots of other tangent lines that you could
write down equations for, but the three shown
here seem to be the easiest.

The original tangent was $y = -\frac{3}{4}x + 6\frac{1}{4}$

The tangent parallel to it is $y = -\frac{3}{4}x - 6\frac{1}{4}$

The reflection of the original tangent in the y-axis
gives $y = \frac{3}{4}x + 6\frac{1}{4}$

The reflection of the original tangent in the x-axis
gives $y = \frac{3}{4}x - 6\frac{1}{4}$

20

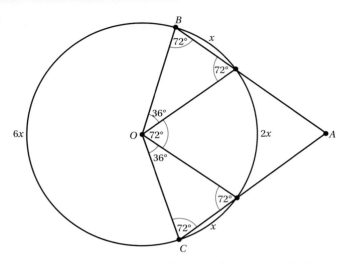

Draw in the radius of the circle. This gives two isosceles triangles.

The total circumference of the circle is $10x$, which means that x is one tenth of the circumference and the angle at the centre of the circle formed by each of the arcs of x is $360 \div 10 = 36°$.

The angle at the centre of the arc of $2x$ is therefore $72°$.

Use the fact that there are isosceles triangles to work out the other angles in those triangles.

Now focus on the biggest quadrilateral in the picture. The angles must add up to $360°$ so angle BAC must be $72°$.

㉑

Triangle **A**

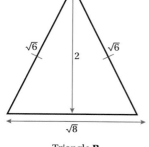

Triangle **B**

The base of the first triangle is $4^{\frac{1}{4}}$ (4 to the power of $\frac{1}{4}$), which is the same as $(4^{\frac{1}{2}})^{\frac{1}{2}}$

This is equal to $\sqrt{2}$.

In Triangle **A** the hypotenuse is $\sqrt{(6)^2 + (2)^2} = \sqrt{8}$

In Triangle **B** the two equal sides are $\sqrt{(4)^2 + (2)^2} = \sqrt{6}$

a The perimeter of Triangle **A** is $\sqrt{8} + \sqrt{6} + \sqrt{2}$

The perimeter of Triangle **B** is $\sqrt{8} + \sqrt{6} + \sqrt{6}$

Because $\sqrt{6} > \sqrt{2}$ Triangle **B** has the bigger perimeter.

b The area of Triangle **A** is $\frac{1}{2}\sqrt{2}\sqrt{6} = \frac{1}{2}\sqrt{12} = \frac{1}{2}\sqrt{4}\sqrt{3} = \sqrt{3}$

The area of Triangle **B** is $\frac{1}{2}\sqrt{8} \times 2 = \sqrt{8}$

Because $\sqrt{8} > \sqrt{3}$ Triangle **B** has the bigger area.

22 **a**

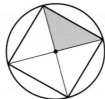

The radius is 1cm so the area of the shaded triangle is $\frac{1}{2}$ and the area of the whole square is 2cm².

You are told the radius of the circle is 1cm, so it makes sense to draw in the radius.

b

The shaded triangle has two sides of 1cm and the angle between them is 120°.

The area, using $\frac{1}{2}ab\sin C$ is $\frac{1}{2}\sin 120$.

The total area of the equilateral triangle is therefore 1.299

The ratio of the area of the triangle to the area of the square is 1.299 : 2

This is 1.299 ÷ 2 : 1 – then multiply by 3 to get 1.9485 : 3, which is approximately 2 : 3

c

The shaded triangle has two sides of 1cm with an angle between them of 72°.

The area, using $\frac{1}{2}ab\sin C$ is $\frac{1}{2}\sin 72$

The total area of the regular pentagon is therefore 2.3776...

Divide this area by the area of the square to get 1.18882... which is approximately $\frac{6}{5}$

1

The two semicircles make a circle, radius 2.25 cm.

Area of circle = π × 2.25² = 15.9043... cm²

Height of triangle = 13 – 2.25 = 10.75 cm

Area of triangle = $\frac{1}{2}$ × 9 × 10.75 = 48.375 cm²

Area of red card = 9 × 13 – 15.9043 – 48.375 = 52.7 cm²
(3 s.f.)

> Start by working out the areas of the different parts of the heart.

> Subtract the areas of the circle and triangle from the area of the rectangle.

2   **a** The diagram shows two wedges. That means 20 of these pairs total a metre long, so x must be 5.

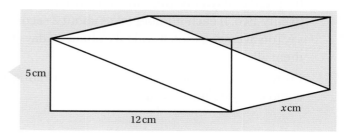

b To make £30 profit and cover the cost of the wood (£5), Ahmed has to take at least £35.

As he has 40 wedges to sell, the minimum cost to achieve this is £35 ÷ 40 = 87.5p.

This rounds to 88p.

3   **a** Principal × 1.08^{10}

= Principal × 2.16

Yes, he would more than double his money.

b £40 000 × 1.08^{10}

£86 357 to the nearest pound

c £30 000 × 1.08^{10} = £64 767.75

£31 000 × 1.08^{10} = £66 926.67

£32 000 × 1.08^{10} = £69 085.60

£33 000 × 1.08^{10} = £71 244.52

£34 000 × 1.08^{10} = £73 403.45

£35 000 × 1.08^{10} = £75 562.37

> 8% interest is an increase with a multiplier of 1.08

> The Principal is the number you begin with (in this case £40 000)

> The bank only gives this deal for £30 000 or more so start checking from this amount.
>
> Another way to work it out is to divide £75 000 by 1.08^{10}.

4   1 000 000 ÷ 60 = 16 666.666... minutes

16666.666... ÷ 60 = 277.777... hours

277.777... ÷ 24 = 11.574 days

Some numbers will be much quicker to say than others. It is quick to say 'three' or 'five hundred thousand', but it takes much longer to say 'two hundred and twenty-two thousand, two hundred and twenty-two'. If each number takes about 2 seconds to say (on average), then it will take about 23 days to say them all.

Even allowing for breaks for sleeping and eating, you could easily do this in your lifetime.

> This method starts by working out how many days is the same as 1 million seconds

Think about what happens when you add odd and even numbers.

Show that:

Even + even = even

Odd + odd = even

Even + odd = odd

Then do the same for multiplication:

Even × even = even

Odd × odd = odd

Even × even × even… = even

Odd × odd × odd… = odd

a $4^3 = 4 \times 4 \times 4 =$ even

$3^4 = 3 \times 3 \times 3 \times 3 =$ odd

Even + odd = odd

So $4^3 + 3^4 =$ odd

An even number raised to any power is even

$(\text{even})^x =$ even

An odd number raised to any power is odd

$(\text{odd})^x =$ odd

b $6^7 =$ even

$3^7 =$ odd

So $6^7 + 3^7 =$ odd

6 $\dfrac{9}{10} \times \dfrac{3}{4} \times \dfrac{1}{3} = \dfrac{27}{120}$

$1 - \dfrac{27}{120} = \dfrac{93}{120}$

This simplifies to give $\dfrac{31}{40}$

A simpler problem would be to work out the probability she doesn't have to stop

You can then work out the probability Helen does have to stop at least once.

159

7 **a**

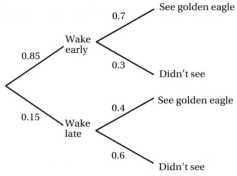

Hamish could see a golden eagle if he wakes up early, but he could also see one if he wakes up later.

$(0.85 \times 0.7) + (0.15 \times 0.4)$

$= 0.655$

b

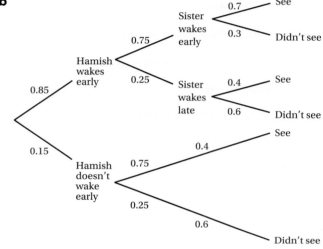

If Hamish wakes up late then it doesn't matter whether his sister wakes up early or late.

$(0.85 \times 0.75 \times 0.7) + (0.85 \times 0.25 \times 0.4) + (0.15 \times 0.4)$

$= 0.59125$

$1 - 0.59125 = 0.40875$

This is the probability that they will see an eagle.

This is the probability that they won't see an eagle.

c $0.655 - 0.591 = 0.064$

The probability goes down from about 0.7 to about 0.6

Without Elspeth, Hamish's chance of seeing a golden eagle is 0.655.

With Elspeth, his chance of seeing a golden eagle is 0.591.

8 **a**

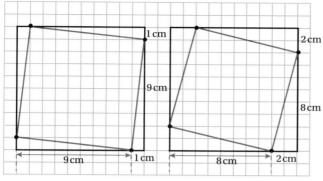

Label what you know. Use the squares on the paper to find the lengths.

$a^2 + b^2 = c^2$ $a^2 + b^2 = c^2$

$9^2 + 1^2 = c^2$ $8^2 + 2^2 = c^2$

$82 = c^2$ $68 = c^2$

$c = \sqrt{82} = 9.055...\text{cm}$ $c = \sqrt{68} = 8.246...\text{cm}$

Now focus on a triangle. Use Pythagoras' theorem to calculate the side length of the titled square.

A line in the first logo is longer than a line in the second logo, so the total line length of the first logo is greater.

b

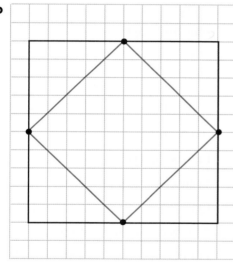

To make a square of half the area you can rotate it.

Calculate the area of the red square by splitting it into triangles. An alternative method would be to use Pythagoras' theorem to find the length of the side of the red square.

a $140 \div 1\frac{1}{2} = 93.3\,\text{km/h}$

b $140 \div 1\frac{1}{3} = 105\,\text{km/h}$

c 10 minutes

d 12 noon

e 4.5 hours, 62.2 km/h

f 3 hours 40 minutes, 76.36 km/h

It is sensible to multiply the number of years by 365 to work out the approximate number of days and to round off the final answer for the following reasons:

- You don't know what time of day they were born, so you don't know whether it is an exact number of days.

- You don't know which month to start with for Ross (some are longer than others).

- You also don't know how many leap years have been involved.

	Shirley	**Ross**	**Jemima**
		169 months	
number of months / 12 = number of years	14.2 years	14.0833333 years	
number of years × 365 = number of days	5183 days	5140.41667 days	5293 days
number of days × 24 = number of hours	124392 hours	123370 hours	127032 hours
number of hours × 60 = number of minutes	7463520 minutes	7402200 minutes	7621920 minutes
number of minutes × 60 = number of seconds	447811200 seconds	444132000 seconds	457315200 seconds
rounded to 3 s.f.	448000000 seconds	444000000 seconds	457000000 seconds

Jemima is the eldest (and is older than Dave by 7 million seconds).

11 Area of **A** is $a\sqrt{2}$.

Area of **B** is $2\sqrt{5} \times \sqrt{10} = 2\sqrt{5} \times \sqrt{5} \times \sqrt{2} = 2 \times 5 \times \sqrt{2} = 10\sqrt{2}$

The areas of the two rectangles are the same, so $a\sqrt{2} = 10\sqrt{2}$ and it is clear that $a = 10$.

> Start by working out what you know.

---

12 $\sqrt{28} \times \sqrt{12}$

$\sqrt{28} \times \sqrt{12} = \sqrt{4} \times \sqrt{7} \times \sqrt{4} \times \sqrt{3} = 4\sqrt{21}$

$\sqrt{7} \times \sqrt{3} = \sqrt{21}$

The fraction that is left is $= \dfrac{3\sqrt{21}}{4\sqrt{21}} = \dfrac{3}{4}$

> Start by working out the area of the bigger rectangle.

> It's easier to simplify this now.

> Now work out the area of the smaller rectangle.

---

13 $V_{\text{hemisphere}}$ is $2\pi r^3 \div 3 = \pi r^3$

V_{cone} is $\pi r^2 h \div 3$

$V_{\text{cone}} = \pi r^2 \div 3 \times 2r = 2\pi r^3 \div 3$

That is the same as for the hemisphere, so the volumes are identical.

> Work out the volume of a hemisphere.

> Work out the volume of a cone.

> The conical hanging basket has a height equal to its diameter. Therefore $h = 2r$.

---

14 **a**

> Work through the information step by step. A table might help.

	12 muffins	30 muffins	fat	sugar
eggs	2	5	$4.6 \times 5 = 23$	trace 0
caster sugar	200 g	500 g		500
milk	250 ml	625 ml	$0.02 \times 625 = 12.5$	$0.05 \times 625 = 31.25$
vegetable oil	125 ml	312.5 ml	312.5	0
flour	400 g	1000 ml	$\dfrac{7}{500} \times 1000 = 14$	$\dfrac{1}{1000} \times 1000 = 1$
salt	1 tsp	2.5 tsp		
			total fat for 30 muffins: 362 g	total sugar for 30 muffins: 532.25 g
			fat for 1 muffin: 12.1 g	**sugar for 1 muffin: 17.7 g**

b Fat: 17% of the GDA

Sugar: 20% of the GDA

15

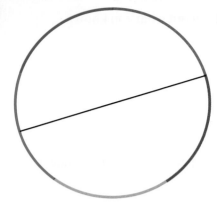

5 of the square fit around the mug, so start with 5 arcs that are the same length around the mug.

The grey line is the diameter (9 cm).

The circumference of the circle is 9π, so each coloured line is = 5.654 867...

The red lines on this square are half of 5.654867.... You can use Pythagoras' theorem to work out the hypotenuse of the right-angled triangle.

= 3.998...

The perimeter is four times this: 15.994 38 = 16.0 cm (3 s.f.).

5 Make changes to the problem

1

a e.g. $\dfrac{1}{50}, \dfrac{1}{49}, \dfrac{1}{48}, \dfrac{1}{47}, \dfrac{1}{46}$

> This question can be answered in many ways, but making changes to the original set of fractions works well.

b e.g. $\dfrac{2}{6}, \dfrac{2}{5}, \dfrac{2}{4}, \dfrac{2}{3}, \dfrac{2}{2}$

c e.g. $\dfrac{6}{2}, \dfrac{7}{2}, \dfrac{8}{2}, \dfrac{9}{2}, \dfrac{10}{2}$

or

$\dfrac{5}{3}, \dfrac{7}{4}, \dfrac{9}{5}, \dfrac{8}{3}, \dfrac{9}{2}$

> You could sprinkle come unrelated fractions around (such as in this final example), but it is easier to work in a systematic way and to make use of some patterns.

2

a $400\,\text{mg} = 0.4\,\text{g}$
$400\,\text{g} + 400\,\text{mg} = 400.4\,\text{g}$

$0.5\,\text{kg} = 500\,\text{g}$
$0.5\,\text{kg} - 90\,\text{g} = 410\,\text{g}$

$400\,\text{g} + 400\,\text{mg} < 0.5\,\text{kg} - 90\,\text{g}$

> Change the quantities so they use the same units. It makes sense to work in grams. $1\,\text{kg} = 1000\,\text{g}$ and $1\,\text{g} = 1000\,\text{mg}$

b $0.1\,\text{km} = 100\,\text{m}$
$150\,\text{cm} = 1.5\,\text{m}$
$0.1\,\text{km} + 150\,\text{cm} = 101.5\,\text{m}$

$900\,\text{cm} = 9\,\text{m}$
$110\,\text{m} - 900\,\text{cm} = 101\,\text{m}$

$0.1\,\text{km} + 150\,\text{cm} > 110\,\text{m} - 900\,\text{cm}$

> Convert everything to metres. $1\,\text{km} = 1000\,\text{m}$ and $1\,\text{m} = 100\,\text{cm}$

c $0.75\,\text{hours} = 45\,\text{minutes}$
$600\,\text{seconds} = 10\,\text{minutes}$
$0.75\,\text{hours} + 600\,\text{seconds} = 55\,\text{minutes}$

$0.1\,\text{hours} = 6\,\text{minutes}$
$50\,\text{minutes} + 0.1\,\text{hours} = 56\,\text{minutes}$

$0.75\,\text{hours} + 600\,\text{seconds} < 50\,\text{minutes} + 0.1\,\text{hours}$

> Convert everything to minutes.

a A diagram shows that 12 chairs are required.

b Every table has 2 chairs, and there are 2 extra on the ends (shown in red).

This means there are $2n + 2$ chairs, where n is the number of tables.

c If it is possible to use 55 chairs then $2n + 2 = 55$, so
$n = 26.5$

Presumably you can't have half a table, so this is not possible.

d Each big group will contain 16 people. $2n + 2$ means that $n = 7$, so each group will require 7 tables and 14 tables will be needed in total.

---

 a $\frac{3}{7}$ of the balls in the bag = 9 balls

$\frac{1}{7}$ of the balls in the bag = 3 balls

The number of balls in the bag = $3 \times 7 = 21$ balls

b $\frac{3}{25}$ of the balls in the bag = 6 green balls

$\frac{1}{25}$ of the balls in the bag = 2 balls

The number of balls in the bag = $2 \times 25 = 50$ balls

$\frac{3}{7}$ of the balls are red and half of the rest are green, which means there are 6 green ones.

---

a Raise 0.9975 to the power of 82 to find out the proportion that will be left after 82 years.

$0.9975^{82} = 0.814\,438$ so 81.4% remains, which means 18.6% has been lost.

Consider the numbers in the question. What happens if you change any of them? The rate of growth of the hair doesn't make a difference to the number of actual hairs that are lost.

The number of strands of hair that people start with doesn't affect the proportion that they lose.

So you just need to look at the proportion that is lost each year.

If you wanted to reduce something by 10% every year then you would instead decide to keep 90% and would multiply by 0.9 for each year.

In this case the average person loses 0.25% per year so they keep 99.75% per year.

b $0.9975^{50} = 0.882\,359$

$0.9975^{40} = 0.904\,724$

$0.9975^{42} = 0.900\,206$

$0.9975^{43} = 0.897\,956$

43 years is the first time it dips below 90%.

If you lose 10% then you have 90% left. You need to know what n is when $0.9975^n \leqslant 0.9$

You can use trial and improvement.

6 **a** $1 + 2 + 3 = 6$, which is 2×3

$2 + 3 + 4 = 9$, which is 3×3

$3 + 4 + 5 = 12$, which is 4×3

$(n - 1) + (n) + (n + 1)$

$n - 1 + n + n + 1 = 3n$

Yes, this is true for all integers.

First, try it out with some more sets of three consecutive integers. You could work systematically.

Once you are convinced that it works, try to think about why.

There are several different ways of explaining this. To start with, think about a general set of three consecutive numbers.

Using algebra you can simplify this expression.

The expression simplifies to $3n$ ($3 \times$ the middle number). So it must be true for all integers.

b $n + (n + 1) + (n + 2) + (n + 3) = 4n + 6$

You could do this algebraically, where n is the first number.

The method for part **b** can be extended for any number of numbers.

c

Number of numbers	Formula, based on the first number being n
2	$2n + 1$
3	$3n + 3$
4	$4n + 6$
5	$5n + 10$
6	$6n + 15$
7	$7n + 21$
8	$8n + 28$

7 To 1 significant figure this calculation is:

$20 \times 800 = 16\,000$, which is about 10 times the size of 1903.02. The answer is likely to be incorrect.

Start with $23.64 \times 805 = 1903.02$

If $23.64 \times 805 = 1903.02$ is true, then:

$2.364 \times 805 = 190.302$

and $2.364 \times 8.05 = 1.90\,302$

The left-hand side must be bigger than 16, so the calculation can't be correct.

---

8 **Snail 1**: $36000\,\text{mm/h}\ (\div 10)$

$3600\,\text{cm/h}\ (\div 60)$

$60\,\text{cm/min}\ (\div 60)$

$1\,\text{cm/s}$

Snail 2: $0.01\,\text{m/s}\ (\times 100)$

$1\,\text{cm/s}$

Snail 3: $5\,\text{km/day}\ (\times 1000)$

$5000\,\text{m/day}\ (\times 100)$

$500\,000\,\text{cm/day}\ (\div 24)$

$20\,833.333\ldots\,\text{cm/h}\ (\div 60)$

$347.222\ldots\,\text{cm/min}\ (\div 60)$

$5.787\ldots\,\text{cm/s}\ (=5.8\,\text{cm/s to 1 d.p.})$

Snail 4: $700\,\text{cm/h}\ (\div 60)$

$11.666\ldots\,\text{cm/min}\ (\div 60)$

$0.19444\ldots\,\text{cm/s}\ (=0.2\,\text{cm/s to 1 d.p.})$

Snail **3** finishes first.

> To compare the snails' speeds they must be measured in the same units.
>
> In this question it might be sensible to convert all the speeds into cm per second (cm/s).

9 **a** Circular pens: C = πd

    Fences with 2 m gap between:

    Inner fence, diameter = 20 m C = 20π

    Outer fence, diameter = 24 m C = 24π

    Difference = 4π

> The formula for the circumference C of a circle with diameter d is C = πd.

b Fences with 3 m gap between:

    Outer fence, diameter = 26 m C = 26π

    Difference = 6π

> Now work out the difference for a 3 m gap between the fences.

c Fences with 4 m gap between:

    Outer fence, diameter = 28 m C = 28π

    Difference = 8π

> Be systematic and work out the difference of a 4 m gap. Can you see a pattern?

The outer fence, diameter = 20 + 2x, C = (20 + 2x)π = 20π + 2πx

> Use algebra to show the general rule.

The difference between this and the inner fence involves subtracting 20π, which leaves 2πx.

d This diagram shows what happens for any rectangles, where the inner one is a by b and there is a gap of x all the way around.

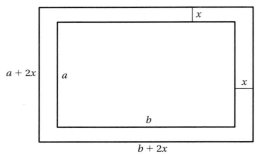

> A square is just a special case of a rectangle with $a = b$

The perimeter of the inner rectangle is $a + b + a + b$ = 2a + 2b

The perimeter of the outer rectangle is (a + 2x) + (b + 2x) + (a + 2x) + (b + 2x) = 2a + 2b + 8x

The difference between these is 8x.

10

$28\,\text{cm} \times 17\,\text{cm} \times 5\,\text{cm} = 2380\,\text{cm}^3$

$21\,\text{cm} \times 15\,\text{cm} \times 9\,\text{cm} = 2835\,\text{cm}^3$

The volume of the BioWheat packet is greater than the volume of the Choc Flakes packet, therefore Mary is wrong.

$2 \times (28 \times 17) + 2 \times (28 \times 5) + 2 \times (17 \times 5) = 1402\,\text{cm}^2$

$2 \times (21 \times 15) + 2 \times (21 \times 9) + 2 \times (15 \times 9) = 1278\,\text{cm}^2$

The surface area of the Choc Flakes packet is greater than the surface area of the BioWheat packet, therefore Kelly is wrong.

Raymon is wrong as the packet with the greater volume does not have the greater surface area.

> Work out the volume and surface area of each packet.

> Volume of Choc Flakes packet.

> Volume of BioWheat packet.

> Conclusion part 1.

> Surface area of Choc Flakes packet.

> Surface area of BioWheat packet.

> Conclusion part 2.

> Conclusion part 3.

---

 11 **a** Daisy can move her shape up and down.

A translation using any vector $\begin{pmatrix} 0 \\ a \end{pmatrix}$ will do this.

> This is a translation where the x-coordinate doesn't change but the y-coordinate can change to be anything.

b A translation using any vector $\begin{pmatrix} a \\ a \end{pmatrix}$ will do this.

> This time Daisy moves her shape diagonally. If she moves it right then she also has to move it up by the same amount.

c

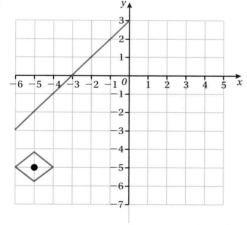

> A good diagram will help here.

To get the black dot onto this line you could use the vector $\begin{pmatrix} a \\ a + 3 \end{pmatrix}$.

> You always need to go up three more than you go across, so the vector will cover all the possibilities (including those with decimals).

12 The perimeter of the large semicircle is $\pi \times \dfrac{6}{2} =$ 9.42... cm

$a^2 = 2^2 + 3^2$

$d = \sqrt{13} = 3.605\,55...$ cm

$\pi \times 3.60655...$ cm $= 11.327...$ cm

Circumference $= \pi \times 3.606\,55...$ cm $= 11.327...$ cm

Total perimeter $= 9.42... + 11.327... = 20.7$ cm (3 s.f.)

> Treat this as a large semicircle and a smaller circle.

> Now find the diameter of the smaller circle.

> This is the hypotenuse of a right-angled triangle.

> The two smaller semicircles have the same circumference as a full small circle.

 13

> To work out the mean of three numbers, add them together and divide by three. As this is a non-calculator question you will need to combine the surds by hand.

> To simplify surds, look for square numbers.

$24 = 4 \times 6$, so $\sqrt{24} = \sqrt{4} \times \sqrt{6} = 2\sqrt{6}$

$54 = 9 \times 6$, so $\sqrt{54} = \sqrt{9} \times \sqrt{6} = 3\sqrt{6}$

Both of these involve 6, so check whether 96 is divisible by 6.

$96 \div 6 = 16$

$96 = 16 \times 6$, so $\sqrt{96} = \sqrt{16} \times \sqrt{6} = 4\sqrt{6}$

This means $\dfrac{\sqrt{24} + \sqrt{54} + \sqrt{96}}{3} = \dfrac{2\sqrt{6} + 3\sqrt{6} + 4\sqrt{6}}{3} = \dfrac{9\sqrt{6}}{3}$
$= 3\sqrt{6}$

---

 14 **a** 1 Try a different starting shape.

2 Try a different pair of perpendicular mirror lines.

3 Try a different starting position for the shape.

b

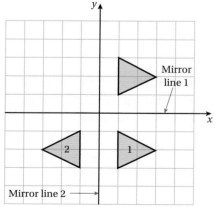

> Mikey has looked at one example and drawn his conclusion based on this.

> If you carry out the reflection in Mikey's chosen mirror lines ($y = 0$ and $x = 0$) with this new shape it becomes clear that something else is happening – the shape has been rotated 180° about the origin.

> Because Mikey's original shape was a rectangle, it has rotational symmetry and he therefore did not notice that the rotation had happened.

> His conclusion was not incorrect, but it was not the full answer. That depends on the nature of the starting shape.

15 **a**

Fraction	Decimal
$\dfrac{1}{9}$	0.1111...
$\dfrac{1}{99}$	0.01010...
$\dfrac{1}{999}$	0.001001001...
$\dfrac{1}{9999}$	0.000100010001...
$\dfrac{1}{99999}$	0.0000100001000010000 1...
$\dfrac{1}{999999}$	0.000001000001...

It seems sensible to use a calculator and to work out the decimal equivalents.

All of the fractions have a denominator that is a multiple of 9.

Similarities

All of the fractions have equivalent decimals that are eventually recurring.

The recurring part of each decimal includes only 1s and 0s.

The number of recurring digits (the period) is the same as the number of digits in the denominator.

The denominator of each fraction is different. In fact the denominator is getting larger with each fraction.

Differences

The equivalent decimal of each fraction is smaller than the previous one.

The number of zeros in the recurring part of the fraction increases with the denominator.

b i $\dfrac{1}{9} = 0.1111...$

Therefore $0.7777... = \dfrac{7}{9}$

Look for similarities between the number and the fractions considered above.

This is similar to the recurring decimal for $\dfrac{1}{9}$. In fact it is seven times bigger.

ii $\dfrac{1}{9} = 0.1111...$

$0.333... = \dfrac{3}{9} = \dfrac{1}{3}$

Therefore $5.3333... = 5\dfrac{1}{3}$

This is also equal to $\dfrac{16}{3}$

iii 0.14444... is the same as 0.44444... − 0.3

$0.44444... = \dfrac{4}{9}$ so you need to do $\dfrac{4}{9} - \dfrac{3}{10}$

This is $\dfrac{40}{90} - \dfrac{27}{90} = \dfrac{13}{90}$

iv 2.5000900090009... is 2.5 + (0.000100010001...)

$\times 9 \div 10$

This is $2\dfrac{1}{2} + \dfrac{9}{99990} = 2\dfrac{1}{2} + \dfrac{1}{11110} = 2\dfrac{5555}{11110} +$

$\dfrac{1}{11110} = 2\dfrac{5556}{11110} = 2\dfrac{2778}{5555}$

16 **a**

Work out angle *A*.

Work out angle *B*.

Work out angle *C*.

Work out angle *D*.

Check whether the angles at *ABC* and *ACB* are equal.

It is possible to work out every angle in the diagram. Start on the left hand side of the diagram.

Base angles in an isosceles triangle are equal.

Angles in a triangle add up to 180°.

Angles on a straight line add up to 180°.

Base angles in an isosceles triangle are equal etc

This will mean the outer triangle is isosceles.

So: Helen is correct.

b Repeating with a starting angle of 10° gives the following triangle.

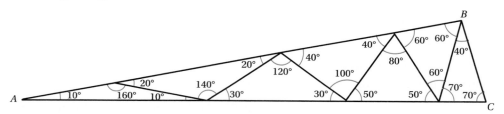

Pete's suggestion of starting with an angle of 10° does not work.

 c

This is an algebraic solution, starting with angle *x*.

Angle $ABC = 6x + 180 - 14x$, which is $180 - 8x$

Angle $ACB = 7x$

These two angles are equal for an isosceles triangle, so $180 - 8x = 7x$, which can be solved to give $x = 12$.

This means that the only starting value that works is 12°.

Draw a diagram to illustrate the situation. This is a problem about similar triangles (the triangle from Jack to the coin and the triangle from Jack to the Moon).

The question says Jack is about 2.5 m away from the coin, so it seems sensible to round off the value for the diameter of the moon to 3500 km.

3500 km = 3 500 000 m = 350 000 000 cm

22.5 mm = 2.25 cm

Calculate the scale factor of enlargement from the coin to the Moon.

Scale factor = 350 000 000 cm ÷ 2.25 = 155 555 555

2.5 m × 155 555 555 = 388 888 889 m

Use the scale factor to enlarge the distance.

Distance to the Moon = 390 000 km (rounded off to 2 s.f.)

1 **a** 12 m × 8 m = 96 m², so the cost is £4 × 96 = £384.

> The first lawn has an area of 80 m² and this costs £320, so each square metre costs £4.
>
> The second lawn has an area of 144 m² and, as expected, the cost is £4 × 144.

b 560 ÷ 4 = 140, so the area is 140 m².

Any pair of integers that multiply to give 140 will work: 1 × 140, 2 × 70, 4 × 35, 5 × 28, 7 × 20, 10 × 14.

---

2 **a** 225 minutes = 3 hours 45 minutes

> A lot of information in the question is irrelevant. The carving time is the same for both birds. The turkey weighs 4.5 kg more, so it needs to be in the oven for 50 minutes × 4.5 longer.

b $t = 50m + 30$

> 5 × 60 + 5 = 305 minutes
>
> (305 − 30) ÷ 50

c 5.5 kg

d 9.25 am if no carving time is required.

9.05 am if 20 minutes of preparation time is needed.

---

3 Clearly this is a joke, but treat is as a question. Make some assumptions about Nick's 'normal' working hours. It might be sensible to assume a working day of 8 hours (9 am – 5 pm).

a 5% of 8 hours is 0.4 of an hour. This doesn't mean very much, so change the 8 hours into minutes. Nick works 8 × 60 minutes = 480 minutes. 5% of this is 24 minutes.

> Calculate the amount of time spent working on Friday.

b One way to do this is to work out that on Wednesday it would be 40% of 480 mins (192 mins) and on Monday 12% of 480 mins (57 mins and 36 seconds). Then subtract to get 134 mins and 24 seconds (2 hours 14 mins 24 seconds).

c It might look as if it must be Nick because he works for 23% compared with Bernard's 18%, but if Bernard's working hours are longer then 18% of a larger amount could be bigger than 23% of a smaller amount.

Do you recognise the equations of perpendicular graphs?

a + 1, –1

b $y = -\frac{1}{2}x - 3$

c The product of the gradients of two perpendicular lines is –1.

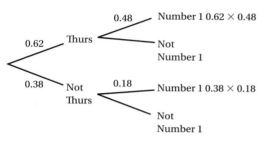

This type of question can be solved using a tree diagram.

The probability of a number one hit is 0.366.

6

Husband		Son
8	57	
9 8 5	58	1 7 8 9 9
5 5	59	1 3 3 4
6 1	60	2 4
3 1	61	
3	62	

Key: 59|4 = 59.4 g

A stem and leaf diagram would be a good way to display the data.

This shows that there are more packets that weigh less than 60 g than packets that weigh 60 g or more.

The median is 59.5 g for her husband and 59.1 g for her son.

It might be better to label the packets as being 59 g instead.

7

	Supermarket A
$\frac{1}{4}$ of the bags	$\frac{1}{4}$ of the bags	$\frac{1}{4}$ of the bags	$\frac{1}{4}$ of the bags

	Supermarket B
$\frac{1}{4}$ of the bags	$\frac{1}{4}$ of the bags	$\frac{1}{4}$ of the bags	$\frac{1}{4}$ of the bags

5   6   7   8   9   10   11   12   13   14

> You don't have enough information to draw a complete box plot, but you can draw the parts for which you do have information.

If there are more apples in the bags then because all the bags weigh 1 kg the apples must weigh less. The biggest apples will presumably be in the bags that have fewer apples in them.

For supermarket B half the bags have 8 apples or fewer, whereas at supermarket A half the bags have 9 apples or fewer. This suggests that the bigger apples are at supermarket B.

But $\frac{1}{4}$ of the bags at supermarket A have 6 apples or fewer, which is better than at supermarket B where $\frac{1}{4}$ of the bags have 7 apples or fewer, so this suggests that the bigger apples are at supermarket A.

8

> It is useful to recognise that a travel graph is likely to help here.

a 10.00

b 5 km

c 7 km

> Draw a graph of the journeys.

> Use the graph to find how far Emma's mum is from Woburn Sands.

d 11.10

e 6 km/h

> Distance = 4 km
>
> Time = 40 minutes = $\frac{2}{3}$ hour
>
> Speed = $\dfrac{\text{distance}}{\text{time}}$

f 5 km

9 **a** 10 km

Use the travel graph to help you answer the questions.

b 20 minutes, 30 km/h (probably driving in town with lower speed restrictions).

c 2 stops, 20 minutes

d Second stage of the journey to Glasgow.

The graph is steepest at this point.

e 80 km in 40 minutes means, means 120 km/h

f 21.05

g approximately 26 km

h 90 km ÷ 3 h = 30 km/h

i 60 km/h

10 $f(x) + 7 = 2x + 4 + 7 = 2x + 11$, which has y-intercept of 11.

This could be explained using algebra.

Alternatively, you could draw a graph.

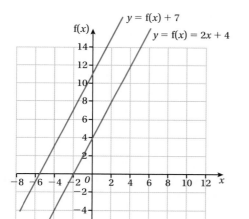

11   **a** All the quickest journeys involve one of the edges
of each length: $4.5\,\text{m} + 3\,\text{m} + 2\,\text{m} = 9.5\,\text{m}$.

   b $GD = \sqrt{(4.5^2 + 2^2)} = 4.92\,\text{m}$

Find *GD* using Pythagoras' theorem.

From *D* to $A = 3\,\text{m}$.

Total distance walked $= 4.92\,\text{m} + 3\,\text{m} = 7.92\,\text{m}$

This is $9.5 - 7.92 = 1.58\,\text{m}$ shorter.

Don't forget to work out the difference between
the two path lengths as this is what was asked for
in the question.

12

You might think that the maximum difference in the
two areas will happen when the area of the circle is
smallest and the area of the square is biggest.

However, the circle is drawn to fit exactly inside
the square so it will always have a diameter equal
to the side length of the square, whatever that is.

Think about the area between the square and the
circle. As the square and circle both get bigger, the
area will get bigger (if this is not clear you could
imagine a very big square/circle and a very small
square/circle).

The upper bound of 7.0 is 7.05 cm.

7.05 cm

The biggest difference between the areas must
happen when you use the upper bound.

$7.05 \times 7.05 = 49.7025\,\text{cm}^2$

Calculate the upper bound for the area of the square.

$\pi \times r^2 = \pi \times \left(\dfrac{7.05}{2}\right)^2 = 39.036...\,\text{cm}^2$

Calculate the area of the circle for the upper
bound of the square side length.

Area of square – area of circle

Calculate the difference between the two areas.

$49.7025\,\text{cm}^2 - 39.036...\,\text{cm}^2 = 10.666...\,\text{cm}^2$

Area of square $= 6.95 \times 6.95 = 48.3025\,\text{cm}^2$

Area of circle $= \pi \times \left(\dfrac{6.95}{2}\right)^2 = 37.936...\,\text{cm}^2$

You can repeat the process with the lower bound of
the square to see that the difference is not as big.

Difference between the two areas $= 10.365...\,\text{cm}^2$.

13 $\sqrt{15}$ is a surd that cannot be simplified, so $10\sqrt{15}$ cannot possibly be an integer. This means C and D must be wrong.

$$10\sqrt{15} = \sqrt{10^2}\sqrt{15} = \sqrt{100 \times 15} = \sqrt{1500}$$

B is correct.

14 **a** 42, 56, 72

b $(n-1) \times n$

This can be written as $n(n-1)$, or as $n^2 - n$.

These numbers have lots of factors. For example:

0	2	6	12	20	30
0×1	1×2	2×3	3×4	4×5	5×6

It is always two consecutive numbers.

c $n(n-1)$ is always a product of two consecutive numbers. One of those two numbers must be even, so the answer must be even too.

15

Work out the volumes of the cylinders.

$8.5 \div 2 = 4.25\,\text{cm}$

Radius of small bottle.

$\pi \times 4.25^2 \times 23 = 1305.14\,\text{cm}^3$ (2 d.p.)

Volume of small bottle (cylinder) = area of circular base × height.

$\pi \times 5.5^2 \times 25 = 2375.83\,\text{cm}^3$ (2 d.p.)

Difference between the volumes of the large and small bottles.

$2375.83 - 1305.14 = 1070.69\,\text{cm}^3$ (2 d.p.)

To the nearest ml, the large bottle holds $1071\,\text{cm}^3$ or $1071\,\text{ml}$ or 1.071 litres more than the smaller bottle.

Conclusion.

16 **a** $\overrightarrow{AB} + \overrightarrow{BC} = \overrightarrow{AC}$

$2a - b - (a + 2b)$

$a - 3b$

b $3(2a - b) = 6a - 3b$

$\overrightarrow{CB} = a + 2b$ and $C_1B_1 = 3a$ so $A_1B_1C_1$ is 3 times bigger than ABC.

Hence A_1B_1 must be 3 times bigger than $\overrightarrow{AB}$

17 **a**

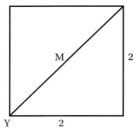

There are lots of ways to do this. One is to work out the length of the diagonal of the square base and then to use this with the slanted height.

Diagonal $= \sqrt{2^2 + 2^2} = \sqrt{8}$

$\sqrt{8} = 2\sqrt{2}$

Use Pythagoras' theorem.

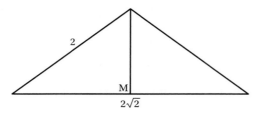

Now use that as the base of an isosceles triangle.

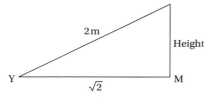

The height of this triangle is the height of the pyramid. You need to halve the $2\sqrt{2}$ to get the base of the triangle.

Height $=$

$\sqrt{2^2 - (\sqrt{2})^2} = \sqrt{4 - 2} = \sqrt{2}$

b height $= \dfrac{3}{2}\sqrt{2}$

You could repeat all the calculations from part **a**, but an alternative is to note that all of the lengths will change in the same way. To turn the 2-pyramid into a 3-pyramid you need to multiply by $\dfrac{3}{2}$.

c height $= \dfrac{n}{2}\sqrt{2}$

To turn the 2-pyramid into an n-pyramid you need to multiply by $\dfrac{n}{2}$.

18 **a**

Height = 18 inches

32 : 18

This simplifies to 16 : 9

In order to calculate the aspect ratio you need to know the height of Carlos' TV.

You know the diagonal length and the width so you need to apply Pythagoras' theorem.

b

The aspect ratio of the TV is 16:9 (width:height)

We know the diagonal length so will have to apply Pythagoras' theorem.

$(9x)^2 + (16x)^2 = 1764$

$337x^2 = 1764$

$x^2 = 1764 \div 337$

$x = \sqrt{1764 \div 337} = 2.287...$ inches

Width = $16x = 16 \times 2.287... = 36.6$ inches (to 1 d.p.)

Height = $9x = 9 \times 2.287... = 20.6$ inches (to 1 d.p.)

19

Triangle ABC is right-angled (because the tongs form a tangent to the circle).

Tan $BAC = \dfrac{2.5}{25}$

Angle $BAC = 5.710\,593$

The angle made by the tongs is double that: 11.421 186

The angle has been reduced by 60 − 11.421 186 = 49° (to the nearest integer).

20   **a** Let t be the number of tables and c be the number of chairs.

$$2t + 2c \leqslant 8$$

b $2t + c \leqslant 6$

c

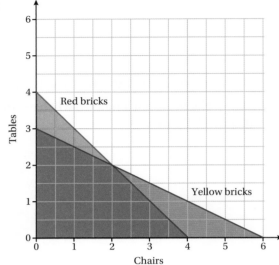

21 **a** You would expect a weak negative correlation.

> It is likely that Year 7 students go to bed earlier and therefore have more sleep than Year 11 students.

b Here is an example:

'Year 11 student have less sleep than Year 7 students.'

c An example:

Question 1: 'What year group are you in?'

Tick one box:

Yr7 ☐ Yr 8 ☐ Yr9 ☐ Yr10 ☐ Yr11 ☐

Question 2: 'On average, how many hours of sleep do you have per night?'

Tick one box

$4\text{hr} < s \leqslant 5\text{hrs}$ ☐

$5\text{hr} < s \leqslant 6\text{hrs}$ ☐

$6\text{hr} < s \leqslant 7\text{hrs}$ ☐

$7\text{hr} < s \leqslant 8\text{hrs}$ ☐

$8+ \text{hrs}$ ☐

d A scatter diagram will show immediately if there is any correlation and possible outliers.

a Upper bound = $1.5 \times 2.5 \times 3.5 = 13.125\,\text{m}^2$

Lower bound = $0.5 \times 1.5 \times 2.5 = 1.875\,\text{m}^2$

Difference is $11.25\,\text{m}^2$

> The biggest volume is calculated using the three upper bounds and the smallest is calculated using the lower bounds.

b Upper bound = $1.005 \times 2.005 \times 3.005 = 6.05515\,\text{m}^2$

Lower bound = $0.9995 \times 1.995 \times 2.995 = 5.97204\,\text{m}^2$

Difference is $0.083\,\text{m}^2$

c Upper bound = $1.0005 \times 2.0005 \times 3.0005 = 6.0055015\,\text{m}^2$

Lower bound = $0.9995 \times 1.9995 \times 2.9995 = 5.9945015\,\text{m}^2$

Difference is $0.011\,\text{m}^2$

 $C = \pi \times \text{diameter}$

> Circumference (C) of dial is πd.

$C = \pi \times (3.2 \times 2) = 6.4\pi\,\text{cm} = 64\pi\,\text{mm}$

> Check the units are the same before dividing.

$121 \div 64\pi\ (= 0.60\ \text{to 2 d.p.})$

The dial has been turned through 0.6 of a turn, which is equivalent to $\frac{3}{5}$.

> Write the arc length as a fraction of the circumference.

This means it ends up pointing at the Wool setting.

---

24 a $\dfrac{3}{\sqrt{5}} = \dfrac{6}{2\sqrt{5}}$

$\dfrac{6}{2\sqrt{5}} > \dfrac{5}{2\sqrt{5}}$

so $\dfrac{3}{\sqrt{5}}$ is larger.

b $\sqrt{8} = \sqrt{(4 \times 2)} = \sqrt{4} \times \sqrt{2} = 2\sqrt{2}$

$\sqrt{50} = \sqrt{(25 \times 2)} = \sqrt{25} \times \sqrt{2} = 5\sqrt{2}$

$\dfrac{4}{\sqrt{8}} = \dfrac{4}{2\sqrt{2}} = \dfrac{2}{\sqrt{2}}$

$\dfrac{25}{\sqrt{50}} = \dfrac{25}{5\sqrt{2}} = \dfrac{5}{\sqrt{2}}$

$\dfrac{2}{\sqrt{2}} < \dfrac{5}{\sqrt{2}}$

so $\dfrac{25}{\sqrt{50}}$ is larger.

c This could be worked out by finding a common denominator for the two fractions like in parts **a** and **b**. An alternative way would be to note that $\dfrac{10}{\sqrt{7}+3}$ is a positive number (because the numerator and the denominator are both positive), but that $\dfrac{6}{\sqrt{7}-3}$ is a negative number (because the numerator is positive but the denominator is negative), so $\dfrac{10}{\sqrt{7}+3}$ is larger.

> In order to compare fractions they need to have the same denominator.

> In order to compare fractions they need to have the same denominator.
>
> It isn't easy to see how to do this for this question. First you must see if you can simplify the surds.

> Now you can see that to find a common denominator you can multiply the top and bottom of the first fraction by 5 and the top and bottom of the second fraction by 2.

 25 a In Shop A the price is £209 instead of £310. This is $\dfrac{209}{310} = 67\%$ of the original price. So the discount is 33%.

Alternatively: Shop A: $\dfrac{310 - 209}{310} \times 100 = 32.58\%$

In Shop B the price is £259 instead of £310. This is $\dfrac{259}{310} = 84\%$ of the original price. So the discount is 16%.

Alternatively: Shop B: $\dfrac{310 - 259}{310} \times 100 = 16.45\%$

b An easy way is to say that the $\dfrac{Shop\ B}{Shop\ A}$ prices for the jacket are $\dfrac{£259}{£209}$. This must be equal to $\dfrac{Shop\ B}{Shop\ A}$ for the shoes.

$\dfrac{£259}{£209} = \dfrac{x}{62}$

so $x = \dfrac{£259}{£209} \times 62 = £76.83$

> There are lots of ways to work this out, including by calculating the original price.

1 **a** $1500\,m \div 200\,m = 7.5$

Simon will need to run 7.5 laps of the indoor running track and 3.75 laps (i.e. 1500 / 400) of the outdoor running track to cover 1500 m.

> Given that the other track is twice as long, he will need half as many laps.

b $5\,km = 5000\,m$

$5000\,m \div 200\,m = 25$

Denise will have to run 25 laps of the indoor track and 12.5 laps of the outdoor track to cover 5 km.

The 10 km is double the 5 km race, so Denise will have to run 50 laps of the indoor track and 25 laps of the outdoor track to cover 10 km.

---

2 **a** $T = 40k + 25$, where k is the number of kilograms.

b Uncle Bertie is wrong; the lamb doesn't need to go into the oven until 9.25 am

> $40 \times 3.75 + 25$ plus an extra 10 minutes of time is 185 minutes. This is the same as 3 hours and 5 minutes.

---

3 **a** Dark chocolate: 675 g

> You need to convert a recipe for 8 people to a recipe that serves 20 people.
>
> You could divide by 8 to find the ingredients for one serving and then multiply by 20.
>
> Alternatively, you could multiply by $\frac{20}{8}$, which is the same as multiplying by $2\frac{1}{2}$.

b 4 bars of 200 g each (because 3 bars is only 600 g)

c $800\,g - 675\,g = 125\,g$

675 : 125

27 : 5

d $\frac{3}{4}$ of 400 g is 300 g.

> To serve 6 people you can divide by 8 and multiply by 6, or you can multiply by $\frac{6}{8}$, which is the same as $\frac{3}{4}$.

4 a

		Day 1		
		Swim	**Jog**	**Cycle**
Day 2	**Swim**	SS	JS	CS
	Jog	SJ	JJ	CJ
	Cycle	SC	JC	CC

This is one way to list all the possibilities in a systematic way.

b $\frac{1}{9}$

c $\frac{6}{9}$ All of the combinations except SS, JJ and CC.

$= \frac{2}{3}$

This is sensible because whichever one is chosen for Day 1, there are 2 out of the 3 that can be chosen on Day 2.

5 a Each cleaner works for 2 hours 45 mins, which is 165 minutes. 5 cleaners work a total of $5 \times 165 = 825$ minutes.

If there are 3 workers then it will take $825 \div 3 = 275$ minutes, which is 4 hours and 35 minutes each.

b 5 cleaners are paid for 3 hours.

3 cleaners are paid for 5 hours.

The total is the same.

6 a Coach Cooksey will have the more accurate mean height as he is using the actual height of each of his members. Coach McKay is finding the estimated mean using the midpoints of each class width. By using the midpoints he is giving each member in each class interval the same height.

Height (cm)	Midpoint	Frequency	Midpoint × frequency
$145 \leqslant h < 155$	150	1	150
$155 \leqslant h < 165$	160	2	320
$165 \leqslant h < 175$	170	2	340
$175 \leqslant h < 185$	180	8	1440
$185 \leqslant h < 195$	190	3	570
$195 \leqslant h < 225$	210	4	840
	Totals:	20	3660

$3660 \div 20 = 183$

b 183 cm

c The mean height is the same for both teams at 183 cm.

But Team Cooksey has both the shortest member (= height 142 cm) and the tallest member (= height 226 cm), so a larger range of heights.

a Glass 1 contains $\frac{1}{4}$ units of squash.

Glass 2 contains $\frac{1}{6}$ units of squash.

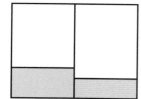

> With questions like this it can help to assign a volume to the glass, be it a numerical value or an algebraic one.
>
> Assume the volume of each glass is 1 unit so that you can just work with the fraction in the question.

Pouring the two glasses together results in a total volume of 2 units.

The squash from glass 1 now represents $\frac{1}{8}$ of the combined drink.

The squash from glass 2 now represents $\frac{1}{12}$ of the combined drink.

$$\frac{1}{8} + \frac{1}{12} = \frac{3}{24} + \frac{2}{24} = \frac{5}{24}$$

So the resulting drink is $\frac{5}{24}$ squash

Notice that this will produce a drink that is weaker than glass 1 and stronger than glass 2.

b The strength of the final drink will be between the two strengths of the original drinks. $\frac{2}{5}$ and $\frac{3}{10}$ are both less than $\frac{1}{2}$ so it is not possible to make a drink that is exactly $\frac{1}{2}$ apple.

---

8 **a** $(x - 6) \times (x - 1)$

$= x^2 - 7x + 6$

So Valerie is correct.

> Area involves multiplying, so it is likely that x^2 will be involved, so Valerie's expression looks more plausible. To work out the area of a rectangle we do length × width.

b and c $x^2 - 7x + 6 - 2 = 2(2x - 7)$

$x^2 - 7x + 4 = 4x - 14$

$x^2 - 11x + 18 = 0$

$(x - 9)(x - 2) = 0$

so $x = 9$ or $x = 2$

If $x = 2$ then one of the sides has negative length (which Doug found funny).

If $x = 9$ then the rectangle is 3 by 8.

9 10% of 90 g = 9 g

$$5\% \text{ of } 90\,\text{g} = \frac{9\,\text{g}}{2} = 4.5\,\text{g}$$

The low fat yoghurt contains more sugar per pot (5.9 g compared to 4.5 g for the 'full fat' version).

$$\frac{5.9\,\text{g}}{90\,\text{g}} = 0.065\,55\ldots$$

$$0.065\,55\ldots \times 100\% = 6.555\ldots\%$$

$$\frac{4.5\,\text{g}}{90\,\text{g}} = 5\%$$

The low fat yoghurt contains approximately 6.6% of the GDA of sugar.

The full fat yoghurt contains 5% of the GDA of sugar.

> Calculate the amount of sugar in grams in the second yoghurt.

> Conclusion

> First consider the low fat yoghurt.

> Next consider the full fat yoghurt.

> Conclusion

10 Grace needs to gain $\frac{5}{95}$ whereas Meg needs to lose $\frac{5}{105}$

$$\frac{5}{95} = 5.263\%$$

$$\frac{5}{105} = 4.762\%$$

> The percentages are not the same even though the amounts of chocolate buttons involved are equal.

11

a $\left(\frac{6}{20}\right)^2 + \left(\frac{5}{20}\right)^2 + \left(\frac{7}{20}\right)^2 + \left(\frac{2}{20}\right)^2 = \frac{114}{400} = \frac{57}{200}$

b $1 - \frac{57}{200} = \frac{143}{200}$

> The easiest way to do this is to realise that picking a different colour the second time is like not picking the same colour.

c $\frac{6}{20} \times \frac{5}{19} + \frac{5}{20} \times \frac{4}{19} + \frac{7}{20} \times \frac{6}{19} + \frac{2}{20} \times \frac{1}{19} = \frac{94}{380} = \frac{47}{190}$

d When he forgets to put the first pen back in the probability that he gets two the same colour goes down.

This makes sense because if green was chosen first and then put back in there is a higher chance green will be picked again than if there were fewer green pens available.

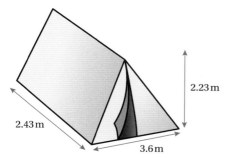

2.23 m

2.43 m

3.6 m

Peter is 2.03 m tall so the tent needs to be at least this long. You might assume that to be comfortable Peter will need the tent to be a little longer, for example at an extra 20 cm at his head and at his feet.

To decide how wide the tent needs to be you have to make an assumption about the 'width' of Peter and his three friends. You want it to be comfortable so you should be generous with your estimate. Perhaps allowing 90 cm per person is reasonable.

Peter also needs to be able to stand up in the tent. If the tent is 2.03 m tall then Peter would just about be able to stand up in the middle (but his head would touch the top). So again, make it more comfortable and given him a little extra room, say 20 cm.

---

13   **a** $£15\,000 = 20\,\text{m}^2 \times k$

$15\,000 \div 20 = k$

$k = £750$ per square metre

$23\,000 \div 750 = 30.666\,666\,\text{m}^2$

But as the area must be an integer value, $a = 30\,\text{m}^2$

b   4 people would take 4 weeks, meaning there are 16 person weeks of work.

To get the job done in 3 weeks there would need to be $16 \div 3 = 5.33\,333$ people. So the builder could employ 5 labourers (making 6 people in total) to finish the job in less than 3 weeks.

Cost = area × constant of proportionality

Rearrange the equation to calculate the value of k.

c The total number of hours is 4 people × 4 weeks × 5 days per week × 9 hours per day = 720 person hours of work.

With 6 people that means each person needs to do 720 ÷ 6 = 120 hours of work.

They work 9 hours per day, which means they need $120 ÷ 9 = 13\frac{1}{3}$ working days.

This is 2 5-day weeks, 3 days and 3 hours. If they start on a Monday they will do two full weeks and will finish on the following Thursday at 11 o'clock.

> Remember, a working day is 9 hours so one third of a working day is 3 hours.

d The 3 hours that the 6 people would need to work on that final day is a total of 18 hours. The builder can do that by himself over two 9-hour days and still finish by the end of the three weeks (assuming there are no jobs that require two people to do them together, such as lifting heavy objects).

e 5 labourers each work 13 days

Total wages = 5 × 13 × £100 = £6500

6500 = 26 parts

One part = 6500 ÷ 26 = 250

Total charge = 90 × 250 = £22 500

Profit = 250 × 25 = £6250

$\frac{6250}{22\,500} × 100 = 27.7777\%$

Job price includes nearly 28% profit.

> This can be answered just by using the ratio.
>
> 26 + 39 + 25 = 90
>
> Percentage charged as profit = $\frac{25}{90} × 100 = 27.8\%$

---

 a Total number of students = 720

$\frac{20}{720} = 0.0278$

Year 7 = 243 × 0.0278 = 6.76, which rounds off to 7 students.

Year 8 = 176 × 0.0278 = 4.89, which rounds off to 5 students.

Year 9 = 162 × 0.0278 = 4.5, which rounds off to 5 students.

Year 10 = 88 × 0.0278 = 2.45, which rounds off to 2 students.

Year 11 = 51 × 0.0278 = 1.42, which rounds off to 1 student.

> Take a stratified sample.

b The stratified sampling method ensures that bigger year groups have more representatives.

Year 11 students are quite important in any school. Only having one Year 11 student on the council might not be a good idea, as that one might not share the same opinions as the majority. Year 7 students are new and might not have mature ideas about particular ideas/needs of older students. Hence for such a council it might be considered best to have 4 students from each year group.

 a Carpet Lay = £85, Underfoot = £105

b Underfoot

c 6 m²

d Underfoot

e £125

> Assume that the lines on the graph continue as straight lines.

 a

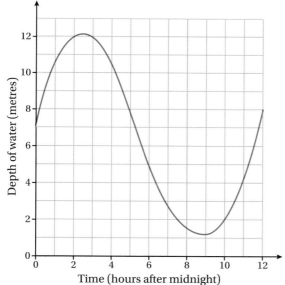

Time (hours after midnight)

b Just after 6 am and just before 11 am (need to read off the graph as accurately as possible).

c Yes, in the second low tide period.

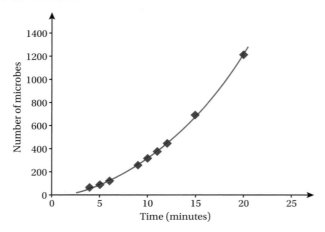

It is sensible to draw a graph.

This graph has a smooth slope, so it can be joined with a curve.

a Reading off the graph at 8 minutes there are about 200 microbes.

b 50 minutes is a long way away from the data, so the pattern might not continue (for example the microbes might get too hot and die off).

---

a

b The missing number in the table is 24.

c On the histogram, to the right of 100 mins there are 8 + 3 = 11 people. Because the data has been grouped you don't know for certain about the 8, but there are at least 3 students who play games for longer than 100 minutes.

---

1 The red cross must be opposite the number 8.

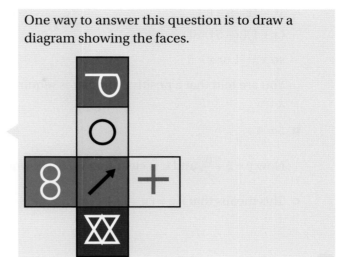

One way to answer this question is to draw a diagram showing the faces.

Another is to spot that the cross appears on the same picture in the question as the P, the O, the arrow and the crossed triangles.

2 It could be a:

triangular prism

triangular-based pyramid

square-based pyramid

cone

other shape

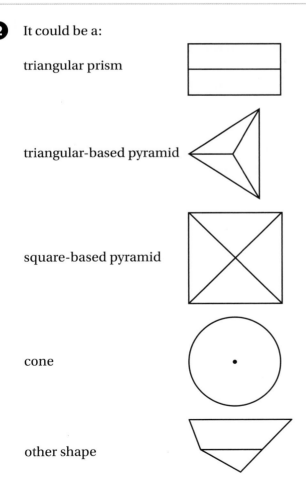

If you are only given the side elevation then there are lots of things it could be. All you know is that there is no 'crease' on that side and it looks like a triangle.

3 **a** $x = 4 + \dfrac{5}{x}$

$x^2 = 4x + 5$

$x^2 - 4x - 5 = 0$

$(x + 1)(x - 5) = 0$

so $x = -1$ or $x = 5$

You are told that a positive number is required, so $x = 5$.

b $5 = 4 + \dfrac{5}{5}$

Now $y = 5 + \dfrac{6}{y}$, and it is clear that $y = 6$ will work.

c This means that if $z = (n - 1) + \dfrac{n}{z}$ then $z = n$.

> You could start with some algebra.

> Multiply by x.

> Factorise.

> Look back on part **a**.

4

> You could draw a few more diagrams and could then make a table of results to see whether that will help you see what is going on (although it won't explain it).

Pattern number	1	2	3	4
Number of metal rods	6	12	18	24
Number of wooden rods	7	12	17	22

a 18

b 22

c $6n$

d The $6 \times 12 = 72$ metal rods will cost £144, and the $5 \times 12 + 2 = 62$ wooden rods will cost £155.

The total cost is £299.

> The number of metal rods goes up by 6 each time because each new panel has 6 metal rods in it.

> The number of wooden rods goes up by 5 each time because when a new panel is added, the left-hand side is joined to the previous panel.

---

5 **a** 80% of £10 is £1 × 8 = £8. 75% of £12 is $\dfrac{3}{4}$ of £12 = £9. 75% of £12 is more money.

b 50% of 1 is a half. 25% of 2 is also $\dfrac{1}{2}$. They are the same.

c We don't need to do any difficult calculations. A 10% discount would be £1.299, which is less than the £1.99 postage charge, so a 5% discount is not enough and it would be cheaper to buy it in the shop.

6

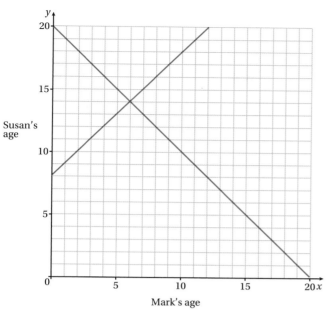

You could draw a graph as in this example solution. An alternative would be to solve the equations.

Their ages total 20, so $x + y = 20$.

Susan is 8 years older than Mark so $y = x + 8$.

The lines cross at $x = 6$ (Mark's age) and $y = 14$ (Susan's age).

7

$a^2 + b^2 = c^2$

$2.1^2 + 1.05^2 = c^2$

$5.5125 = c^2$

$c = \sqrt{5.5125} = 2.347... \,\text{m}$

2.4 metres is more than the height of the door. Even when it is tilted it will be a close-run thing as to whether it will fit.

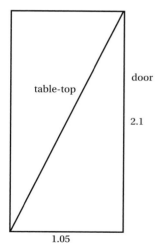

Arthur's new table has a diameter of 240 cm. Even if Arthur turns the table to try to go through the door diagonally, it will not fit because it is more than 5 cm too big.

197

a You know it is inversely proportional, so it must look like this:

$$y = \frac{k}{x}$$

$$20\,000 = \frac{k}{4}$$

$$k = 80\,000$$

A possible formula is: number of bacteria =

$$\frac{80\,000}{\text{number of hours}}$$

b $\frac{80\,000}{8} = 10\,000$

c There will be problems when the time is very small. At zero hours it doesn't work at all.

 a The blue graph is MoveIt Builders, the red line is JCE.

b MoveIt Builders = £15

c £14

> £70 for 5 days, daily rate = £70 ÷ 5

d Less, £12, £2 per day

> MoveIt Builders 75 for 5 days (75 − 15 = 60, 60 ÷ 5)

e £75

f £183

> 15 + (12 × 14)

g MoveIt Builders

> 14 × 14 = 196

h £13 cheaper

10 **a**

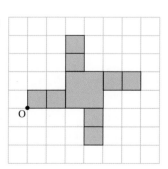

b 0 lines of symmetry

c rotational symmetry order 4

d 1 Draw a circle of radius 1 cm.

> There are several ways this image could be created. Here is one possible set of instructions.

   2 Enlarge this circle by a scale factor of 2 about the centre of the circle.

   3 Translate the small circle 2 cm to the left.

   4 Translate the small central circle 2 cm to the right.

11 $f(x) = (x - 2)(x + 2) = x^2 - 4$

You could answer this question algebraically.

The translation vector $\begin{pmatrix} 0 \\ 4 \end{pmatrix}$ moves the graph up by 4 on the y-axis. Algebraically this can be explained as:

$f(x) = (x - 2)(x + 2) + 4$

$f(x) = x^2 + 2x - 2x - 4 + 4$

$f(x) = x^2$

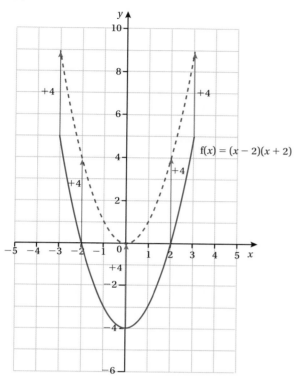

Both of these methods show that she is correct.

12 **a** and **b**

You don't know how many hamsters there are, or how many cages, which makes this difficult.

$h = 3c + 1$ and $h = 4(c - 1)$

You could write two equations and then solve them (using h for the number of hamsters and c for the number of cages).

An alternative would be to use some diagrams.

The three hamsters from the final cage, and the extra one, have been shared out and put into the other cages. That means there are now 4 cages with 4 hamsters each and one empty cage.

There are 5 cages and 16 hamsters.

a If three consecutive even numbers add up to 228 then the middle one is half of 228, the smallest one is 2 less than that and the biggest one is 2 more.

This gives 76 as the middle number so the answers are:

74, 76, 78

b Similar reasoning gives the middle number as 291 ÷ 3 = 97.

The three numbers are 95, 97, 99.

c Half of 1301 is 650.5, so the two numbers must be either side of . This is 25.504... so the two numbers are 25 and 26.

> You could make a quadratic using $x^2 + (x + 1)^2 = 1301$ and solve it. An alternative would be to look for a rough average, as in this example.

d If the two numbers were equal then they would each be 40 (because their sum is 80). To get a difference of 6 you need to subtract 3 from one and add 3 to the other, giving 37 and 43.

> Alternatively you could make two equations and solve them (e.g. $x - y = 6$ and $x + y = 80$).

 a $\frac{2}{3}$ as a decimal is 0.666... so $\frac{2}{3} > 0.66$.

> It is much easier to compare them if they are both fractions or are both decimals.

b $0.25 = \frac{1}{4}$

$\frac{8}{32} = \frac{1}{4}$, so $0.25 = \frac{8}{32}$

> In this pair, the fraction can actually be simplified. This will make the comparison easier.

c $\frac{3}{11} = 0.272727...$

so $\frac{3}{11} < 0.273$

> Use short division to evaluate the decimal equivalent to $\frac{3}{11}$.
>
> In this question it is easier to compare the decimals (finding a common denominator to compare the fractions is not as easy).

d $0.05 = \frac{5}{100} = \frac{1}{20}$,

$\frac{1}{20} > \frac{1}{22}$, so $0.05 > \frac{1}{22}$

e Here is a diagram showing 0.49.

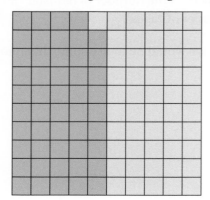

Now if you shade 0.4999 of the shape you get this (there is a tiny part of that top square which hasn't been shaded):

(Note that if you keep on doing this you get closer and closer to 0.5 each time, so you say that 0.4999 … = 0.5)

15 **a** If a to the power of something = 1 then the power equals zero.

$(a^x)^y = a^{xy}$, so either $x = 0$ or $y = 0$. The other one can be anything.

The only exception is if $a = 1$, when x and y can be anything.

b $(a^x)^y = a^1$ means that $x \times y = 1$.

> You may find that there are some other restrictions. For example, if a is zero or negative.

c $(a^x)^y = \sqrt{a}$ means that $x \times y = \frac{1}{2}$

16 $150\,000\,\text{ml} \div 1000\,\text{ml} = 150$ bottles

> Work out how many bottles of cola are required.

$150 \times £1.49 = £223.50$

> Work out the total cost of the cola.

$150\,000 \div 400 = 375$ tins

> Compare that with the number of tins of beans.

$375 \times 54\text{p} = £202.50$

> Work out the total cost of the beans.

A quicker way would be to say that 1 ml of beans costs 54p ÷ 400 = 0.135p/ml, whereas 1 ml of cola costs 149p ÷ 100 = 0.149p/ml so the beans are cheaper.

17

$4x^2 - 12x + 9 = (2x - 3)(2x - 3)$

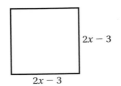

This is helpful because it means the sides of the square are all $2x - 3$. The perimeter is therefore $4(2x - 3)$ or $8x - 12$.

This involves several steps. Start with what you know: the square has area $4x^2 - 12x + 9$.

Usually you would square root the area to work out the length of a side. If you don't know how to square root the algebra you could factorise it.

 18 a

This is one way to split up the shape.

The top rectangle has area: $2(3x - 4) = 6x - 8$

The left rectangle has area: $2(2x - 5) = 4x - 10$

Altogether all four rectangles add up to $20x - 36\,\text{cm}^2$

b $20x - 36 = 204$

$20x = 240$

$x = 12$

This means $3x$ is 36 and $(2x - 5)$ is 19.

The dimensions are 36 cm by 19 cm.

 19 a The first number is each product is n and the second one is $3n - 1$.

The nth term is therefore $n(3n - 1)$ or $3n^2 - n$.

b 234 is divisible by 9, so work out $234 \div 9 = 26$

Those two numbers work: $9 \times 26 = 234$

Knowing the factors of 234 is helpful here.

20 **a** $4x + 5y = 205$ (equation 1)

$3x + 7y = 235$ (equation 2)

Let x be the price of each apple in pence, and y be the price of each banana in pence.

b and **c**

One way to solve this is to get the same number of xs in each equation.

$12x + 28y = 940$

Multiply equation 2 through by 4

$12x + 15y = 615$

Multiply equation 1 through by 3

$13y = 325$

Subtract

$y = 25$

Divide by 13

This means a banana costs 25 pence.

$4x + 5 \times 25 = 205$

Substitute $y = 25$ into equation 1.

$4x = 80$

$x = 20$ so an apple costs 20 pence.

d

You use the intersection of the two lines to find the cost of an apple and a banana.

---

21 **a**

A Venn diagram will help to show what is going on.

Fill the 17 in first.

Then use the information about how many people own a dog.

Then use the information about how many people own either a dog or a cat but not both.

Finally, fill in the ones who own neither a dog nor a cat.

$\frac{29}{100}$

b $\frac{41}{100}$

22 **a** 24.6 : 24

246 : 240

123 : 120

b The ratios of times is 123 : 120, whatever units are used.

> You could start again, having converted the times to minutes, but these ratios don't have units.

c $6.4 \times 10^{23} : 6.0 \times 10^{24}$

64 : 600

8 : 75

d 27 : 9

3 : 1

> The two mountains are approximately 27 km and 9 km tall.

23 **a**

8 ⟶ 14

1 ⟶ 14 ÷ 8

20 ⟶ $y = 14 \div 8 \times 20$

> Find the value of y and then use the formula for the area of a triangle.

Triangle ABC has area 80 cm².

Triangle XYZ has area 245 cm².

b The ratio is 80 : 245, which simplifies to 16 : 49.

c 16 and 49 are both square numbers.

The ratio of the sides is 4 : 7.

The ratio of the areas is $4^2 : 7^2$.

24 **a** There are two possibilities:

Rotate **A** 180° about (0,3)

Enlarge **A** by a scale factor of –1 about point (0,3)

b There are a lot of possibilities:

Do two reflections (e.g. in the line $x = 0$ and then in the line $y = 3$).

Do a rotation and a translation (e.g. rotate A 180° about (–2,3) and then translate it 4 units to the right.

Do a translation and then a rotation, or two enlargements, or an enlargement and a translation.

25

a

x	-2	-1	0	1	2	3	4	5	6
$f(x)$	11	2	-5	-10	-13	-14	-13	-10	-5

b The turning point is at (3, -14).

Drawing a graph might help.

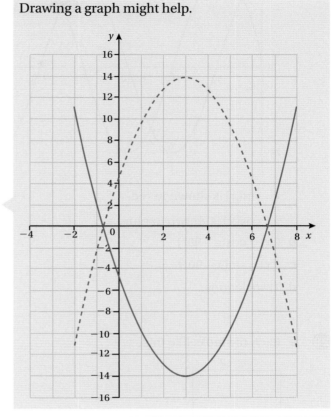

c $x^2 - 6x - 5 = 0$

$(x - 3)^2 - 9 - 5 = 0$

$(x - 3)^2 - 14 = 0$

$(x - 3)^2 = 14$

$x - 3 = \pm\sqrt{14}$

$x = 3 \pm \sqrt{14}$

The graph only gives approximate versions of where it crosses the x-axis. You could complete the square or use the formula to get these answers.

d The graph of $y = -f(x)$ shows that the turning point is at (3, 14)

e This is the same as part **c**.

26

a $f(x - 8)$ moves the original function to the right by 8, whereas the vector moves it down by 8.

b The vector to move right by 8 is $\begin{pmatrix} 8 \\ 16 \end{pmatrix}$.

If this is not clear then you could draw graphs of $y = f(x)$ and $y = f(x - 8)$.

27 **a**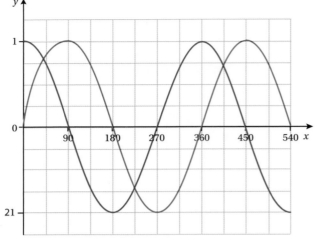

$y = \sin(x)$ is shown in red.

$y = \cos(x)$ is shown in blue.

b $f(x) = \cos(x - 90°)$

c $f(x) = \sin(x + 90°)$

d Translations.

---

28 **a** Each tile looks like this:

The area is $(3x - 2)(x - 1) = 3x^2 - 5x + 2$

Four of them have area $= 12x^2 - 20x + 8$

b The big square has sides of $4x - 3$, so the area is
$(4x - 3)^2 = 16x^2 - 24x + 9$

c $4x^2 - 4x + 1$

$(2x - 1)^2 = 4x^2 - 4x + 1$

To work out the inner square's area you can subtract part **a** from part **b**.

Or you could see on the diagram that the side of the inner square is $2x - 1$.

29 **a** The area of the semicircle is $\pi \times 25 \div 2 =$ 39.269... cm^2 – this is not the same as Ollie's answer of 39.3 cm^2.

$\sqrt{75} = 8.660...$ cm – this is not the same as Ollie's answer of 8.7 cm.

Ollie has rounded too early in each calculation.

> There are lots of things that might have gone wrong. You could work through Ollie's calculations and check the following:
>
> Did he use the radius and not the diameter?
>
> Did he halve the area of the circle?
>
> Did he subtract when using Pythagoras' theorem?
>
> Did he work out the area of the triangle incorrectly?

b $12.5\pi + 5\sqrt{75} = 82.571...$ cm^2, which is 82.6 cm^2 to 1 d.p.

---

30 **a** For the triangles to be similar they must have the same angles. The paper is square so the corners are all 90°.

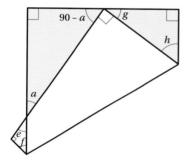

> Let the angles in the larger triangle be a and $90 - a$.

for smaller triangle: $a = e$

> Vertically opposite angles are equal.

$f = 90 - a$

> Angles in a triangle add up to 180°.

So the angles in the smallest triangle are: $a, 90, 90 - a$.

$b = 90 - a$

> Angles in a triangle add up to 180°.

So the angles in the top left triangle are: $a, 90, 90 - a$

Along the top line:

> Angles on a straight line.

$90 - a + 90 + g = 180$

so $g = a$

$h = 90 - a$

> Angles in a triangle add up to 180°.

The angles in the final triangle are $a, 90, 90 - a$.

The angles in the three triangles are identical so the triangles are similar.

b The square has sides of 8 cm so you know that $CG + BG = 8$, $CE + ED = 8$, and AC and CB are both 4.

You can work out that $BG = 3$ and $CG = 5$ using Pythagoras:

$CG^2 = BG^2 = 4^2$

but $CG = 8 - BG$ so $(8 - BG)^2 = BG^2 + 16$

$64 - 16BG + BG^2 = BG^2 + 16$

$48 = 16BG$

$BG = 3$

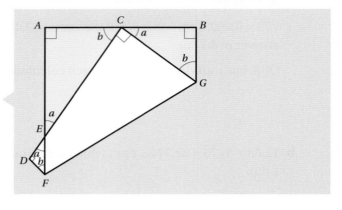

Move between thinking about each right-angled triangle to thinking about the square.

You know from part **a** that all the triangles are similar, so $\dfrac{CE}{CG} = \dfrac{AC}{BG}$

$CE = \dfrac{4}{3} \times 5 = \dfrac{20}{3} = 6\dfrac{2}{3}$,

and $\dfrac{AE}{BC} = \dfrac{AC}{BG}$

$AE = \dfrac{4}{3} \times 4 = \dfrac{16}{3} = 5\dfrac{1}{3}$

$DE = 8 - 6\dfrac{2}{3} = 1\dfrac{1}{3}$

$\dfrac{AE}{DE} = 5\dfrac{1}{3} \div 1\dfrac{1}{3} = \dfrac{16}{3} \div \dfrac{4}{3} = 4$, so the sides of the largest triangle are 4 times those of the smallest one.

a

Work out the other lengths on the diagram.

The height of the triangle can be worked out using Pythagoras' theorem:

$$\sqrt{1^2 - \left(\frac{1}{2}\right)^2} = \sqrt{\left(\frac{3}{4}\right)} = \frac{\sqrt{3}}{2}$$

i $\quad \tan 60° = \dfrac{opp}{adj} = \dfrac{\sqrt{3}}{2} \div \dfrac{1}{2} = \sqrt{3}$

ii $\quad \sin 60° = \dfrac{opp}{hyp} = \dfrac{\sqrt{3}}{2} \div 1 = \sqrt{3}$

iii $\quad \cos 60° = \dfrac{adj}{hyp} = \dfrac{1}{2} \div 1 = \dfrac{1}{2}$

b $\quad$ To work out $\sin 60°$ you need $\dfrac{\sqrt{3}}{2} \div 1 = \dfrac{opp}{hyp}$

To work out $\cos 30°$ you need $\dfrac{\sqrt{3}}{2} \div 1 = \dfrac{adj}{hyp}$

The opposite side needed to work out $\sin 60°$ is the adjacent side needed to work out $\cos 30°$.

The same argument holds true for $\sin 30°$ and $\cos 60°$.

1 **a**

+	1	2	3	4	5	6	7	8	9
1									
2									
3									
4									
5									
6									
7									
8									
9									

Pair up every integer with every other integer systematically.

The table illustrates all the possible calculations that can be made.

Notice that these are different calculations. They do not necessarily represent different answers.

If you want to assume that 2 + 5 is a different calculation from 5 + 2 then you need all 81 cells, otherwise you only need the shaded ones.

b

	-9	**-8**	**-7**	**-6**	**-5**	**-4**	**-3**	**-2**	**-1**
-9	-18	-17	-16	-15	-14	-13	-12	-11	-10
-8	-17	-16	-15	-14	-13	-12	-11	-10	-9
-7	-16	-15	-14	-13	-12	-11	-10	-9	-8
-6	-15	-14	-13	-12	-11	-10	-9	-8	-7
-5	-14	-13	-12	-11	-10	-9	-8	-7	-6
-4	-13	-12	-11	-10	-9	-8	-7	-6	-5
-3	-12	-11	-10	-9	-8	-7	-6	-5	-4
-2	-11	-10	-9	-8	-7	-6	-5	-4	-3
-1	-10	-9	-8	-7	-6	-5	-4	-3	-2

The red cells show the 17 different answers you can get.

---

2 $+ - \times$ $5 + 2 - 10 \times 3 = 5 + 2 - -30 = 5 + 2 + 30 = 37$

Make a systematic list of the arrangements of the three operations and then calculate the answers.

$+ \times -$ $5 + 2 \times 10 - -3 = 5 + 20 + 3 = 28$

$- + \times$ $5 - 2 + 10 \times -3 = 5 - 2 - 30 = -27$

$- \times +$ $5 - 2 \times 10 + -3 = 5 - 20 - 3 = -18$

$\times + -$ $5 \times 2 + 10 - -3 = 10 + 10 + 3 = 23$

$\times - +$ $5 \times 2 - 10 + -3 = 10 - 10 - 3 = -3$

You can achieve a negative result in three different ways.

3 **a** **i**

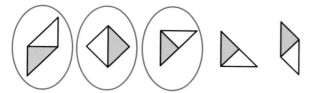

With two sandwiches it is possible to create three polygons: a right-angled isosceles triangle, a parallelogram and a square.

If you have two sandwiches (two triangles) then it might make sense to keep one of them fixed and move the other around it. Here the blue one is fixed and the white one moves.

There are three different positions in which the second sandwich could be placed.

ii

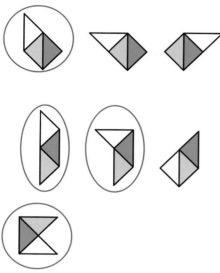

With three sandwiches it is possible to create four polygons: two different trapeziums and two different irregular pentagons.

If you have three sandwiches (three triangles) then it makes sense to start with the three arrangements for two sandwiches and move the third sandwich around these.

The second and third ones are congruent to the first one – and the others that start with a square will also all be congruent.

The third one is congruent to the ones above. All the others that start with the parallelogram will be congruent to others that we have already got.

This is the only new one.

Conclusion

iii

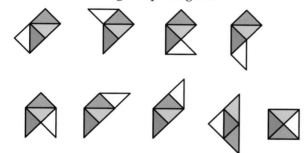

With four sandwiches it is possible to create nine polygons: a rectangle, four different irregular hexagons, an isosceles trapezium, a parallelogram, an isosceles triangle and a square.

b Yes.

If you have four sandwiches (four triangles) then it makes sense to start with the four arrangements for three sandwiches and move the fourth sandwich around these.

Again, some of these are identical or are reflections of each other.

These are the ones that are distinct.

This is almost a trick question. A square is an example of all the special quadrilaterals (it is also a rectangle, a parallelogram, a rhombus, a kite and a trapezium), so the original sandwich works for all of them.

4 **a** If a and b are not negative and have to be whole numbers then either $a = 1$ and $b = 0$ or $a = 0$ and $b = 1$.

   b This time they are positive, so 0 cannot be used.

   1   $0.1 + 0.9 = 1$

   2   $0.2 + 0.8 = 1$

   3   $0.3 + 0.7 = 1$

   ...

   9   $0.9 + 0.1 = 1$

> There are 9 of them.

   c 1 $0.01 + 0.99 = 1$

   2   $0.02 + 0.98 = 1$

   3   $0.03 + 0.97 = 1$

   ...

   9   $0.99 + 0.01 = 1$

> There are 99 of them.

   d If a and b are allowed to be negative then $a + b = 1$ without any restrictions and there are infinite possibilities.

5

$$\frac{2}{3} + \frac{1}{5} = \frac{10}{15} + \frac{3}{15} = \frac{13}{15}$$

$$\frac{2}{3} - \frac{1}{5} = \frac{7}{15}$$

$$\frac{1}{5} - \frac{2}{3} = -\frac{7}{15}$$

$$\frac{2}{3} \times \frac{1}{5} = \frac{2}{15}$$

$$\frac{2}{3} \div \frac{1}{5} = \frac{2}{3} \times \frac{5}{1} = \frac{10}{3}$$

$$\frac{1}{5} \div \frac{2}{3} = \frac{1}{5} \times \frac{3}{2} = \frac{3}{10}$$

   a The biggest answer is $\frac{10}{3}$

   b The smallest answer is $-\frac{7}{15}$

6　**a**　Box 1: four cylinders of radius 10 cm and height 15 cm

Box 2: one cylinder of radius 20 cm and height 15 cm

Box 3: sixteen cylinders of radius 5 cm and height 15 cm

b　Students' guesses

c　Box 1: volume of cylinders = $\pi \times 10^2 \times 15 \times 4 = 6000\pi$

Box 2: volume of cylinders = $\pi \times 20^2 \times 15 = 6000\pi$

Box 3: volume of cylinders = $\pi \times 5^2 \times 15 \times 16 = 6000\pi$

Because the total volume of the cylinders is the same each time the unused space is the same in each box.

> Did this answer surprise you? Or did you guess that all three boxes had the same amount of unused space?
>
> If you look at each calculation for the volume of the cylinders, you will notice that each has $\pi \times 15$. The rest of the calculation for each volume multiplies to give the same answer, 400.
>
> $4 \times 10^2 = 20^2 = 16 \times 5^2 = 400$

7　**a**

> There are two Jacks and because they are different suits it is useful to call them J_1 and J_2.

		second card			
		J_1	J_2	Q	K	A
first card	J_1		J_1J_2	J_1Q	J_1K	J_1A
	J_2			J_2Q	J_2K	J_2A
	Q				QK	QA
	K					KA
	A					

b　Of these 10 possibilities 1 involves the two jacks: $\frac{1}{10}$

c　From the table it is $\frac{3}{10}$

8 **a** _ _ _ _ 3 3 _ _ _ _

> The median is 3, and because the mode of 10 numbers is 3 and there are only three different numbers, there must be at least four 3s. The mean is 6, so the total is 60.

3 3 3 3 3 3 _ _ _ 13 and the other numbers must be 8, 8, 13.

> The range is 10, so if the lowest number is 3 you get this.

> If the lowest is 2 then the highest is 12 and there are no combinations of 2, 3 and 12 that fit the rules.

1 3 3 3 3 3 11 11 11 11 works.

> If the lowest is 1 then the highest is 11.

b 3 3 3 71

1 3 3 73 will work

> The mode and the median are both 3 so the middle two numbers are both 3. The mean is 20 so they all add up to 80.

> The mode is 3 so there must be at least two 3s. The median is 5, so you get this.

c 3, 3, 7, 67

d 3, 3, 17, 57

e 3, 3, 27, 47

f As long as two of the numbers are 3 and the other two are both odd and add up to 74 then this will work.

---

9 **a** The number 1 is used in four lines. So is the number 2.

> As an alternative method, you could add up the totals for each line.

All the numbers from 1 to 7 are used four times so the total is $(1 + 2 + 3... + 7) \times 4 = 28 \times 4 = 112$.

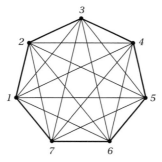

b In a hexagon each number joins to three others, so the total is $(1 + 2 + 3... + 6) \times 3 = 21 \times 3 = 63$

In a pentagon each number joins to two others, so the total is $(1 + 2 + 3 + 4 + 5) \times 2 = 15 \times 2 = 30$

The total of $63 + 30 = 93$ is less than 112.

10 **a** This table shows there are 78 pairs of numbers.

	1	2	3	4	5	6	7	8	9	10	11	12
1	1	1	1	1	1	1	1	1	1	1	1	1
2	1	2	1	2	1	2	1	2	1	2	1	2
3	1	1	3	1	1	3	1	1	3	1	1	3
4	1	2	1	4	1	2	1	4	1	2	1	4
5	1	1	1	1	5	1	1	1	1	5	1	1
6	1	2	3	2	1	6	1	2	3	2	1	6
7	1	1	1	1	1	1	7	1	1	1	1	1
8	1	2	1	4	1	2	1	8	1	2	1	4
9	1	1	3	1	1	3	1	1	9	1	1	3
10	1	2	1	2	5	2	1	2	1	10	1	2
11	1	1	1	1	1	1	1	1	1	1	11	1
12	1	2	3	4	1	6	1	4	3	2	1	12

b The number in each cell is the HCF of the pair of numbers. The co-prime numbers are shown with a 1. This is $\frac{46}{78} = \frac{23}{39}$

11 You know that all powers of 1 are 1, so this means that $2^b + 3^c = 244$.

You don't need to worry about negative powers of 2 and 3 because they will give fractions.

You could make a list of powers of 2 and powers of 3, but consider for a moment that 3^c is always odd. The only way to get an even result (like 244) is for 2^b to be odd.

So this must be $2^0 = 1$ and $3^c = 243$

> The only way 2^b can be an odd number is if $b = 0$

3^0	1
3^1	3
3^2	9
3^3	27
3^4	81
3^5	243

This means that:

a can be anything

$b = 0$

$c = 5$

You know the triangles are equilateral because the sides are all radii of the circles. This helps to work out the angle of 240°.

There are many ways to work this out. This method uses two sectors of circles (shown unshaded) and two equilateral triangles.

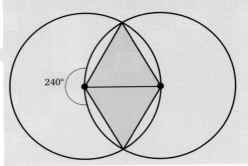

The perimeter is therefore: $\frac{240}{360} \times \pi \times d \times 2 = \frac{16}{3}\pi$.

The area of each sector is $\frac{240}{360} \times \pi r^2 = \frac{8}{3}\pi$.

The area of one triangle is $\frac{1}{2}ab\sin C = \frac{1}{2} \times 2 \times 2 \times \sin 60°$.

The total area is therefore $\frac{16}{3}\pi + 2\sqrt{3}$

The cost of the pool is $\frac{16\pi}{3} \times £225 + (\frac{16\pi}{3} + 2\sqrt{3})\, £800 =$ £19 945

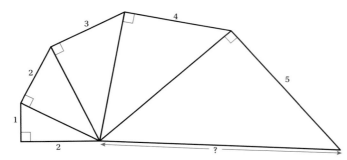

Use Pythagoras' theorem in the smallest triangle, but leave your answer as a surd because you will need to square it again to work out the hypotenuse of the second triangle, and so on.

The final hypotenuse is the square root of $2^2 + 1^2 + 2^2 + 3^2 + 4^2 + 5^2$

This is $\sqrt{59}$

End of week number	1	2	3	4	5	6
Number of people	4	16	64	256	1024	4096

She gives the mixture away at the end of each week, so this table shows the number of people who have the mixture at the end of the week. Because each person shares theirs with 3 others it is multiplied by 4 each week.

a 256 people will have it after 4 weeks.

b 4096 people after 6 weeks.

c $4^{13} = 67\,108\,864$

So 13 weeks are required.

d Not everyone will pass it on or keep their own one going. Babies and children would find it difficult. After a while everyone you know will have it and you won't be able to find anyone new to pass it on to.

15

N	Fraction	Decimal	Recurring or terminating?
1	$\frac{1}{1}$	1	Terminating
2	$\frac{1}{2}$	0.5	Terminating
3	$\frac{1}{3}$	0.3333...	Recurring
4	$\frac{1}{4}$	0.25	Terminating
5	$\frac{1}{5}$	0.2	Terminating
6	$\frac{1}{6}$	0.1666...	Recurring
7	$\frac{1}{7}$	0.142857142857...	Recurring
8	$\frac{1}{8}$	0.125	Terminating
9	$\frac{1}{9}$	0.1111...	Recurring
10	$\frac{1}{10}$	0.1	Terminating

Four of the fractions $\frac{1}{N}$, where N is any positive integer from 1 to 10, are recurring.

If the numerator is 1 then the terminating ones must have denominators whose only prime factors are 2 or 5.

1 **a** Jyoti's tower = 1 + 2 + 3 + 4 + 5 + 6 = 21 cm

Indira's tower = 7 + 8 + 9 + 10 + 11 + 12 = 57 cm

Indira's tower is 36 cm taller.

b 57 + 21 = 78 cm

One possible answer is 1 + 2 + 3 + 10 + 11 + 12 = 39

and 4 + 5 + 6 + 7 + 8 + 9 = 39

> The total height of all the cubes is 78 cm.
>
> 78 ÷ 2 = 39 cm gives the height when they are the same.
>
> Each girl must now have a combination that is 39 cm high.

2 **i** False

> The last digit, 2, is even so the number is even.

ii True

> If you add the digits of the number together you get 48, which is divisible by 3, so the number is also divisible by 3.

iii False

> The number is a multiple of 3, so it cannot be prime. It is also even.

iv True

> The number 12345678910 is in the 5 times table, so if you divide 12345678912 by 5 then the remainder is 2.

v True

> The last two digits are 12, which is a multiple of 4, so the number is a multiple of 4. Tip: if a number is a multiple of 4 then the last two digits will be also be a multiple of 4.

3 Grandad's age is $2x$, Geoff's age is x and Paul's age is $x - 29$.

> One way to do this is to call Geoff's age x and to work out the other ages in terms of x.

In total this is $2x + x + x - 29$, which equals 131.

$4x - 29 = 131$, so $4x = 160$ and $x = 40$.

The ages are: Grandad is 80, Geoff is 40 and Paul is 11.

4 Call the daughter's age x. The father is then $5x$ and the mother is $5x - 9$.

Adding these up gives $11x - 9$, which is equal to 134 years.

Solve $11x - 9$ to get $x = 13$.

The mother is therefore $5 \times 13 - 9 = 56$ years old.

---

5 **a** $1 : 8$

    $x : 140$

    $140 \div 8 = 17.5$

    18 teachers

Ratio of teachers to students.

Let number of teachers = x.

Number of teachers must be a whole number.

b $21 \times 8 = 168$

    $168 - 140$

    28 more students

Every adult can have 8 students to supervise.

A total of 168 students can go.

Number of extra students.

c $21 : 140$

    $3 : 20$

    roughly $1 : 7$

Teachers : students.

d $140 : 25$

    $28 : 5$

First find the number of coaches needed.

21 teachers + 140 students = 161 seats needed.

$4 \times 42 = 168$ seats.

So 4 coaches are needed.

4 coaches need 4 drivers.

Total adults = 25.

Students : Adults.

$140 : 25$

e $\dfrac{25}{165} = \dfrac{5}{33}$

Total adults = 25.

Total in the group = $25 + 140 = 165$.

6

A clear, well-labelled diagram will be useful. This one focuses on the important triangle.

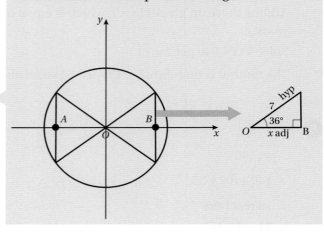

$OB = \cos 36° \times 7\,\text{cm} = 5.663...\,\text{cm}$

To work out x you need to use trigonometry.

B: (5.66, 0)

Now interpret this in terms of the coordinates of point B (values rounded up to 2 d.p. as required).

A: (–5.66, 0)

Point A is a reflection of point B in the y axis.

7

You know the following:

There are eight numbers.

The biggest is 16.

The range is 15, so the smallest is 16 – 15 = 1.

The mean is 7.5 so they all add up to 7.5 × 8 = 60

The mode is 3 and 5 so there are the same number of 3s and 5s, and there must be two or three of each.

The six numbers that must be included are 1, 3, 3, 5, 5, 16 and the others must be between 1 and 16. These ones add up to 33 so the other two add up to 27.

a and b The possible solutions are therefore:

1, 3, 3, 5, 5, 12, 15, 16

1, 3, 3, 5, 5, 13, 14, 16

---

8 **a** The mode is 2 and the median is 5 so there must be:

2 2 5 _ _

The range is 15 so the biggest one is 17 and the mean is 7 so they all need to total 35, giving 9 as the other number:

2, 2, 5, 9, 17

b For the range, mode and median from before there has to be 2 2 5 _ 17

These total 26. The mean is an integer so the total must be a multiple of 5. The biggest number that is allowed in the space is 16 but this gives 42 altogether so it must be 14 and the mean is 8.

c This time the mean is not stated to be an integer. 2, 2, 5, 6, 17 gives the smallest mean of $32 \div 5 = 6.4$

9 **a** If $c = 1$ then:

$3 = \dfrac{2}{1} + 1$

$3 = \dfrac{4}{2} + 1$ etc

If $c = 0$ then:

$3 = \dfrac{3}{1} + 0$

$3 = \dfrac{6}{2} + 0$ etc

If $c = 2$ then:

$3 = \dfrac{a}{b} + 2$ works for anything where $a = b$ (except zero).

If $c = 3$ then:

$3 = 0 + 3$ works for $a = 0$ and anything except $b =$ zero.

These solutions also work if both **a** and **b** are negative.

b and **c** In these two final scenarios b can be greater than 1 or less than zero.

10

0.74 or $\frac{74}{100}$	0.46 or $\frac{46}{100} = \frac{23}{50}$	0.9 or $\frac{90}{100} = \frac{9}{10}$
0.86 or $\frac{129}{150} = \frac{43}{50} = \frac{86}{100}$	0.7 or $\frac{70}{100} = \frac{7}{10}$	0.54 or $\frac{54}{100} = \frac{27}{50}$
0.5 or $\frac{50}{100} = \frac{1}{2}$	0.94 or $\frac{94}{100} = \frac{47}{50}$	0.66 or $\frac{33}{50} = \frac{66}{100}$

Remember that in a magic square all the rows and columns and both main diagonals add up to the magic number. The key idea here is to convert everything into the same type of number. It is easiest to work in either decimals or in fractions with a denominator of 100. The diagram shows possible answers: you only need one answer in each square.

11 There are four aces, so the probabilities are:

$\frac{4}{52} \times \frac{3}{51} = \frac{12}{2652}$

You could start by writing down the probability of picking one ace. Then, if you are lucky and have picked an ace, write down the probability of picking an ace when there are only 51 cards left.

There are two red kings, so the probabilities are:

$\frac{2}{52} \times \frac{1}{51} = \frac{2}{2652}$

Picking two aces is 6 times as likely.

12

		Socks						
		G	**G**	**B**	**B**	**B**	**BLU**	**STR**
Ties	**P**	a	a					
	BLU					d		
	PUR							b
	G	c d	c d					

In probability questions a diagram of some kind is often helpful.

a $\frac{2}{28} = \frac{1}{14}$

b $\frac{1}{28}$

c $\frac{2}{28} = \frac{1}{14}$

d $\frac{3}{28}$

e $1 - \frac{3}{28} = \frac{25}{28}$

a $1 - (0.1 + 0.2 + 0.3 + 0.3)$

    0.1

b $0.1 \times 0.1 = 0.01$

c p(4 kits and 6 kits) = $0.1 \times 0.3 = 0.03$

    p(5 kits and 5 kits) = $0.2 \times 0.2 = 0.04$

    p(6 kits and 4 kits) = $0.3 \times 0.1 = 0.03$

    Any of these outcomes are possible, so add them together to get 0.1

> The probabilities should add up to 1.

> A table might help, but note that this shows the different possibilities and not the probabilities (because they are not all equally likely).

+	4	5	6	7	8
4			10		
5		10			
6	10				
7					
8					16

 1 pint (imperial) is 0.568 litres (568 ml).

9 pints = 568 ml × 9 = 5112 ml

5112 ml = approximately 5000 ml

= 5×10^3 ml of blood in James' body.

There are 5×10^9 red blood cells per millilitre of blood, so in total James has about $5 \times 10^9 \times 5 \times 10^3$

= $25 \times 10^{12} = 2.5 \times 10^{13}$ red blood cells

10% of $2.5 \times 10^{13} = 0.25 \times 10^{13}$

The number of remaining blood cells is
$2.5 \times 10^{13} - 0.25 \times 10^{13} = 2.25 \times 10^{13}$

> We know there are two different units in the question: millilitres and pints.

> Here we have converted pints into millilitres.

> The question asks you to work with approximate figures.

15 **a**

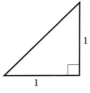

$\sqrt{1^2 + 1^2} = \sqrt{2}$

So the hypotenuse is $\sqrt{2}$.

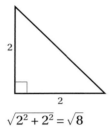

$\sqrt{2^2 + 2^2} = \sqrt{8}$

So the hypotenuse is $\sqrt{8}$.

These numbers are both used in the question.

However, the second triangle has sides that are double those of the first triangle.

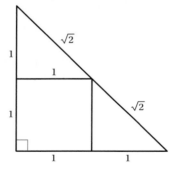

So $2\sqrt{2} = \sqrt{8}$

b $3\sqrt{2}$ looks like a triangle with sides 3 times those of the small triangle.

It seems sensible to work out the length of each hypotenuse (because square roots are involved).

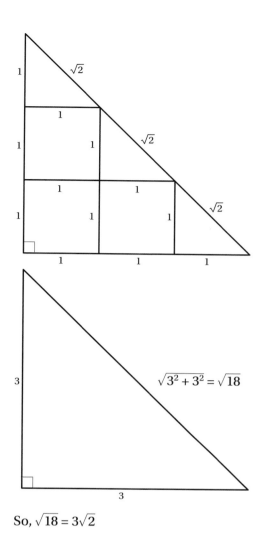

So, $\sqrt{18} = 3\sqrt{2}$

16 **a** $30x + 20y \leqslant 350$

> Each glass of lemonade needs 30 g sugar, so altogether the drinks needs 30x sugar.
>
> Each brownie need 20 g sugar, so altogether the snacks need 20y sugar.
>
> In total this must be less than or equal to 350.

b Let n be number of friends.

$50n \leqslant 350$

so $n \leqslant 7$

> If everyone has one of each, then that is 50 g per person.

a

The usual way to work out the median from a grouped frequency table is to draw a cumulative frequency graph.

Weekly (£)	Frequency	Cumulative Frequency
61–80	2	2
81–100	5	7
101–150	9	16
151–200	2	18
201–250	1	19
251–300	1	20

This gives a median of about £116, which is not helpful to the manager as it is below £130.

b The median won't increase.

You might be interested to see what happens to the median when worked out in this way!

The mean salary is $(7 \times 90.5 + 9 \times 125.5 + 2 \times 175.5 + 1 \times 225.5 + 1 \times 275.5) \div 20$

This is £130.75, so you could say that the average is now above the national average.

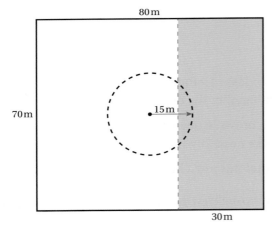

This is not easy to visualise, so a sketch is a good idea.

You need to know the shaded area that the goat can reach.

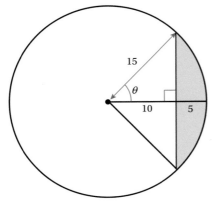

The angle is worked out by doing $\cos\theta = \frac{10}{15}$

so $\theta = 48.189...$

The area of the sector is $\frac{2\theta}{360} \times \pi \times 15^2$

The area of the triangle is $\frac{1}{2}ab\sin C = \frac{1}{2} \times 15 \times 15 \times \sin(2\theta)$

This gives the shaded, goat-eaten area as $189.24... - 111.80... = 77.437...$

The cost of planting the wheat is $30 \times £65 = £1950$

The takings are $£4.50 \times (30 \times 70 - 77.437...) = £9101.53$

The farmer's profit is $£9101.53 - £1950 = £7151.53$

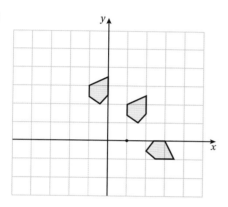

It seems sensible to work backwards through the transformations.

The question isn't clear as to whether the second, intermediate diagram is drawn, so you might not have the one near the middle of the diagram.

20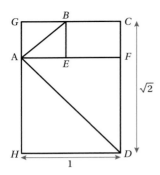

This question can be answered in lots of ways. Here is one that does not involve the use of Pythagoras' theorem.

The question states that it is a kite, so $AD = CD$ and $AB = BC$.

AD and CD are both $\sqrt{2}$.

$AH = 1$

Because it is folded across the width of the rectangle, which is 1.

so $GA = \sqrt{2} - 1$

GA is folded to meet AE so $AE = (\sqrt{2} - 1)$ and $EF = 1 - (\sqrt{2} - 1) = 2 - \sqrt{2}$

BC is the same as EF, so sides AB and BC are both $2 - \sqrt{2}$

The four sides total: $\sqrt{2} + \sqrt{2} + 2 - \sqrt{2} + 2 - \sqrt{2} = 4$

21

$KE = \frac{1}{2}mv^2$, where m is the mass in kg and v is the speed in m/s.

The first thing you might want to do is to try to work this out for yourself.

The tennis ball has mass 56 g and velocity 120 miles per hour.

$56\,g = 0.056\,kg$ so $m = 0.056$

120 miles per hour = $120 \times \frac{8}{5}$ km per hour = 192 km per hour

$v = \frac{192\,000}{3600}$ m/s $= 53.\dot{3}$ m/s

$KE = \frac{1}{2} \times 0.056 \times (53.\dot{3})^2$

$= 79.6$ Joules

Student 1 has not converted the units so that the mass is in kg and the speed is in mph.

Student 2 appears to have worked out $(\frac{1}{2}mv)^2$ rather than $\frac{1}{2}mv^2$ (where only the v should be squared).

CAMBRIDGE

Brighter Thinking

GCSE
MATHEMATICS
online

The complete online resource for GCSE Mathematics

GCSE Mathematics Online for Edexcel is our brand new interactive teaching and learning subscription service. This tablet-friendly resource supports both independent learning and whole class teaching through a suite of flexible resources that includes lessons, tasks, questions, quizzes, widgets and games.

▸ Allows teachers to set tasks and tests, auto-mark and compile reports to review student performance.

▸ A test generator so teachers can compile their own assessments.

▸ Interactive widgets to visually demonstrate concepts.

▸ Worksheets offering practical activities, discussion points, investigations, games and further practice.

▸ Walkthroughs that take students through a question step-by-step, with feedback.

▸ Quick-fire quizzes with leaderboards, providing an opportunity for question practice.

▸ Levelled questions that assess understanding of each topic.

▸ Covers both Foundation and Higher, offering flexibility for moving students between tiers.

▸ Resources organised into chapters corresponding to the Student Books, with explanatory notes for all topics.

▸ Contains material for all types of classroom set-up, including interactive whiteboards and projectors.

www.gcsemaths.cambridge.org